THE OPEN SEA

THE OPEN SEA

By

EDGAR LEE MASTERS

𝖓𝖊𝖜 𝖄𝖔𝖗𝖐
THE MACMILLAN COMPANY
1921

All rights reserved

COPYRIGHT, 1921,
BY THE MACMILLAN COMPANY.

Set up and electrotyped. Published November, 1921.

Press of
J. J. Little & Ives Company
New York, U. S. A.

CONTENTS

PART I

[v]

CONTENTS

THE OPEN SEA

PART ONE

THE OPEN SEA

BRUTUS

BRUTUS AND ANTONY

(Lucilius Talks at a Feast Given to Aristocrates in Rome.)

B. C. 20

THE OPEN SEA

BRUTUS

BRUTUS AND ANTONY

Part I

(Lucilius Talks at a Feast Given to Aristocrates in Rome)

B. C. 20

How shall I write this out? I do not write.
Talk to you? Yes, and tell of Antony,
And how I knew him.   There at Philippi
I let myself be captured, so to give
Time to escape to Brutus—made pretense
That I was Brutus, and so Brutus flies
And I am captured.   Antony forgives me,
And to his death I was his faithful friend.
Well, after Actium, in Africa,
He roamed with no companions but us two,
Our friend Aristocrates, here, myself,
And fed upon his bitter heart.   Our guest
Nods truth to what I say, he knows it all.
And after certain days in solitude

[3]

BRUTUS AND ANTONY

He seeks his Cleopatra. As for her,
She was the sovereign queen of many nations;
Yet that she might be with her Antony,
Live with him and enjoy him, did not shun
The name of mistress, and let Fulvia keep
Her wifehood without envy. As for him,
A lover's soul lives in the loved one's body,
And where bode Cleopatra, there his soul
Lived only, though his feet of flesh pursued
The Parthian, or Cæsar's hateful heir. . . .
And if this Antony would wreathe his spear
With ivy like a thyrsus; from the chamber
Of his beloved rush to battle, helmet
Smelling of unguents and of Egypt; leave
Great action and great enterprise to play
Along the seashore of Canopus with her;
And fly the combat, not as Paris did,
Already beaten, with lift sail, desert
The victory that was his, yet true it is
His rank, his eloquence, his liberal blood,
His interest in all grades and breeds of men,
His pity and his kindness to the sick,
His generous sympathies, stamped Antony
A giant in this dusty, roaring place
Which we call earth. Who ruined Antony?
Why, Brutus! For he gave to Antony
The truth of which the Queen of Egypt stood
As proof in the flesh:—Beauty and Life. His heart
Was apt to see her for mad days in Rome,

[4]

BRUTUS AND ANTONY

And soul created sateless for the cup
Of ecstasy in living.

                    On a day
Myself and Aristocrates and Antony,
We two companioning him in Africa,
Wandering in solitary places, Antony
Brooding on Actium, and the love that kept
His soul with Cleopatra, up he speaks,
And asks us if we knew what Brutus said,
While nearing death, to Cassius. "No," we said.
And Antony began to tell of Brutus:—
How all his life was spent in study, how
He starved his body, slept but briefly, cut
His hours of sleep by practice; fixed his thought
On virtue and on glory; made himself
A zealot of one purpose: liberty;
A spirit as of a beast that knows one thing:
Its food and how to get it; over its spirit
No heaven keeps of changing light; no stars
Of wandering thought; no moons that charm
Still groves by singing waters, and no suns
Of large illumination, showing life
As multiform and fathomless, filled with wings
Of various truth, each true as other truth.
This was that Brutus, made an asp by thought
And nature, to be used by envious hands
And placed to Cæsar's breast. So Antony
Discoursed upon our walk, and capped it off
With Brutus' words when dying. They were these:

[5]

"O virtue, miserable virtue, bawd and cheat;
Thou wert a bare word and I followed thee
As if thou hadst been real.   But even as evil,
Lust, ignorance, thou wert the plaything too
Of fortune and of chance."
        So Antony
Consoled himself with Brutus, sighed and lapsed
To silence; thinking, as we deemed, of life
And what it yet could be, and how 'twould end;
And how to join his Cleopatra, what
The days would hold amid the toppling walls
Of Rome in demolition, now the hand
Of Cæsar rotted, and no longer stayed
The picks and catapults of an idiot world!
So, as it seemed, he would excuse himself
For Actium and his way in life.   For soon
He speaks again, of Theophrastus now,
Who lived a hundred years, spent all his life
In study and in writing, brought to death
By labor; dying lay encompassed by
Two thousand followers, disciples, preachers
Of what he taught; and dying was penitent
For glory, even as Brutus was penitent
For virtue later.   And so Antony
Spoke Theophrastus' dying words, and told
How Theophrastus by a follower
Asked for a last commandment, spoke these words:
"There is none.   But 'tis folly to cast away
Pleasure for glory!   And no love is worse

[6]

BRUTUS AND ANTONY

Than love of glory. Look upon my life:—
Its toil and hard denial! To what end?
Therefore live happy; study, if you must,
For fame and happiness. Life's vanity
Exceeds its usefulness."
                              So speaking thus
Wise Theophrastus died.
                              Now I have said
That Brutus ruined Antony. So he did,
If Antony were ruined—that's the question.
For Antony hearing Brutus say, "O virtue,
Miserable virtue, bawd and cheat," and seeing
The eyes of Brutus stare in death, threw over him
A scarlet mantle, and took to his heart
The dying words of Brutus.

                              It is true
That Cicero said Antony as a youth
Was odious for drinking-bouts, amours,
For bacchanals, luxurious life, and true
When as triumvir, after Cæsar's death,
He kept the house of Pompey, where he lived,
Filled up with jugglers, drunkards, flatterers.
All this before the death of Brutus, or
His love for Cleopatra. But it's true
He was great Cæsar's colleague. Cæsar dead,
This Antony is chief ruler of all Rome,
And wars in Greece, and Asia. So it's true
He was not wholly given to the cup,

But knew fatigue and battle, hunger too,
Living on roots in Parthia. Yet, you see,
With Cæsar slaughtered in the capitol,
His friend, almost his god; and Brutus gasping
"O miserable virtue"; and the feet of men
From Syria to Hispania, slipping off
The world that broke in pieces, like an island
Falling apart beneath a heaving tide—
Whence from its flocculent fragment wretches leap—
You see it was no wonder for this Antony,
Made what he was by nature and by life,
In such a time and fate of the drifting world,
To turn to Cleopatra, and leave war
And rulership to languish.
                                        Thus it was:
Cæsar is slaughtered, Antony must avenge
The death of Cæsar. Brutus is brought to death,
And dying scoffs at virtue which took off
In Brutus' hand the sovran life of Cæsar.
And soon our Antony must fight against
The recreant hordes of Asia, finding here
His Cleopatra for coadjutor. . . .
He's forty-two and ripe. She's twenty-eight,
Fruit fresh and blushing, most mature and rich;
Her voice an instrument of many strings
That yielded laughter, wisdom, folly, song,
And tales of many lands, in Arabic,
And Hebrew, Syriac and Parthiac.
She spoke the language of the troglodytes,

BRUTUS AND ANTONY

The Medes and others. And when Antony
Sent for her in Cilicia, she took time,
Ignored his orders, leisurely at last
Sailed up the Cydnus in a barge whose stern
Was gilded, and with purple sails. Returned
His dining invitation with her own,
And bent his will to hers. He went to her,
And found a banquet richer than his largess
Could give her. For while feasting, branches sunk
Around them, budding lights in squares and circles,
And lighted up their heaven, as with stars.
She found him broad and gross, but joined her taste
To him in this. And then their love began.
And while his Fulvia kept his quarrels alive
With force of arms in Rome on Octavianus,
And while the Parthian threatened Syria,
He lets the Queen of Egypt take him off
To Alexandria, where he joins with her
The Inimitable Livers; and in holiday
Plays like a boy and riots, while great Brutus
Is rotting in the earth for Virtue's sake;
And Theophrastus for three hundred years
Has changed from dust to grass, and grass to dust!
And Cleopatra's kitchen groans with food.
Eight boars are roasted whole—though only twelve
Of these Inimitable Livers, with the Queen
And Antony are to eat—that every dish
May be served up just roasted to a turn.
And who knows when Marc Antony may sup?

[9]

Perhaps this hour, perhaps another hour,
Perhaps this minute he may call for wine,
Or start to talk with Cleopatra; fish—
For fish they did together. On a day
They fished together, and his luck was ill,
And so he ordered fishermen to dive
And put upon his hook fish caught before.
And Cleopatra feigned to be deceived,
And shouted out his luck. Next day invited
The Inimitable Livers down to see him fish,
Whereat she had a diver fix his hook
With a salted fish from Pontus. Antony
Drew up amid their laughter. Then she said:
"Sweet Antony, leave us poor sovereigns here,
Of Pharos and Canopus, to the rod;
Your game is cities, provinces and kingdoms."
Were Antony serious, or disposed to mirth?
She had some new delight. She diced with him,
Drank with him, hunted with him. When he went
To exercise in arms, she sat to see.
At night she rambled with him in the streets,
Dressed like a servant-woman, making mischief
At people's doors. And Antony disguised
Got scurvy answers, beatings from the folk,
Tormented in their houses. So it went
Till Actium. She loved him, let him be
By day nor night alone, at every turn
Was with him and upon him.

BRUTUS AND ANTONY

                            Well, this life
Was neither virtue, glory, fame, nor study,
But it was life, and life that did not slay
A Cæsar for a word like Liberty.
And it was life, its essence nor changed nor lost
By Actium, where his soul shot forth to her
As from a catapult a stone is cast,
Seeing her lift her sixty sails and fly.
His soul lived in her body as 'twere born
A part of her, and whithersoever she went
There followed he. And all their life together
Was what it was, a rapture, justified
By its essential honey of realest blossoms,
In spite of anguished shame. When hauled aboard
The ship of Cleopatra, he sat down
And with his two hands covered up his face!
Brutus had penitence at Philippi
For virtue which befooled him. Antony
Remorse and terror there at Actium
Deserting with his queen, for love that made
His body not his own, as Brutus' will
Was subject to the magic of a word. . . .
For what is Virtue, what is Love? At least
We know their dire effects, that both befool,
Betray, destroy.

             The Queen and Antony
Had joined the Inimitable Livers, now they joined
The Diers Together. They had kept how oft

BRUTUS AND ANTONY

The Festival of Flagons, now to keep
The Ritual of Passing Life was theirs.
But first they suffered anger with each other
While on her ship, till touching Tenarus
When they were brought to speak by women friends,
At last to eat and sleep together. Yet
Poison had fallen on their leaves, which stripped
Their greenness to the stalk, as you shall see. . . .
Here to make clear what flight of Antony meant,
For cause how base or natural, let me say
That Actium's battle had not been a loss
To Antony and his honor, if Canidius,
Commanding under Antony, had not flown
In imitation of his chief; the soldiers
Fought desperately in hope that Antony
Would come again and lead them.

                              So it was
He touched, with Cleopatra, Africa,
And sent her into Egypt; and with us,
Myself and Aristocrates, walked and brooded
In solitary places, as I said.
But when he came to Alexandria
He finds his Cleopatra dragging her fleet
Over the land space which divides the sea
Near Egypt from the Red Sea, so to float
Her fleet in the Arabian Gulf, and there,
Somewhere upon earth's other side, to find
A home secure from war and slavery.

BRUTUS AND ANTONY

She failed in this; but Antony leaves the city,
And leaves his queen, plays Timon, builds a house
Near Pharos on a little mole; lives here
Until he hears all princes and all kings
Desert him in the realm of Rome; which news
Brings gladness to him, for hope put away,
And cares slipped off. Then leaving Timoneum,—
For such he named his dwelling there near Pharos—
He goes to Cleopatra, is received,
And sets the city feasting once again.
The order of Inimitable Livers breaks,
And forms the Diers Together in its place.
And all who banquet with them, take the oath
To die with Antony and Cleopatra,
Observing her preoccupation with
Drugs poisonous and creatures venomous.
And thus their feast of flagons and of love
In many courses riotously consumed
Awaits the radiate liquor dazzling through
Their unimagined terror, like the rays
Shot from the bright eyes of the cockatrice,
Crackling for poison in the crystal served
By fleshless hands! A skeleton steward soon
Will pass the liquer to them; they will drink,
And leave no message, no commandment either—
As Theophrastus was reluctant to—
Denied disciples; for Inimitable Livers
Raise up no followers, create no faith,
No cult or sect. Joy has his special wisdom,

Which dies with him who learned it, does not fire
Mad bosoms like your Virtue.

                            I must note
The proffered favors, honors of young Cæsar
To Cleopatra, if she'd put to death
Her Antony; and Antony's jealousy,
Aroused by Thyrsus, messenger of Cæsar,
Whom Cleopatra gave long audiences,
And special courtesies; seized, whipped at last
By Antony, sent back to Cæsar. Yet
The queen was faithful. When her birth-day came
She kept it suitable to her fallen state,
But all the while paying her Antony love,
And honor, kept his birth-day with such richness
That guests who came in want departed rich. . . .

Wine, weariness, much living, early age
Made fall for Antony. October's clouds
In man's life, like October, have no sun
To lift the mists of doubt, distortion, fear.
Faces, events, and wills around us show
Malformed, or ugly, changed from what they were.
And when his troops desert him in the city
To Cæsar, Antony cries out, the queen,
His Cleopatra, has betrayed him. She
In terror seeks her monument, sends word
That she is dead. And Antony believes
And says delay no longer, stabs himself,

[14]

BRUTUS AND ANTONY

Is hauled up dying to the arms of her,
Where midst her frantic wailings he expires!
Kings and commanders begged of Cæsar grace
To give this Antony his funeral rites.
But Cæsar left the body with the queen
Who buried it with royal pomp and splendor.
Thus died at fifty-six Marc Antony,
And Cleopatra followed him with poison,
The asp or hollow bodkin, having lived
To thirty-nine, and reigned with Antony
As partner in the empire fourteen years. . . .

Who in a time to come will gorge and drink,
Filch treasure that it may be spent for wine,
Kill as Marc Antony did, war as he did,
Because Marc Antony did so, taking him
As warrant and exemplar? Why, never a soul!
These things are done by souls who do not think,
But act from feeling. But those mad for stars
Glimpsed in wild waters or through mountain mists
Seen ruddy and portentous will take Brutus
As inspiration, since for Virtue's sake
And for the good of Rome he killed his friend;
And in the act made Liberty as far
From things of self, as murder is apart
From friendship and its ways. Yes, Brutus lives
To fire the mad-men of the centuries
As Cæsar lives to guide new tyrants. Yet
Tyrannicide but snips the serpent's head.

BRUTUS AND ANTONY

The body of a rotten state still writhes
And wriggles though the head is gone, or worse,
Festers and stinks against the setting sun. . . .

Marc Antony lived happier than Brutus
And left the old world happier for his life
Than Brutus left it.

AT THE MERMAID TAVERN

(*April 10th, 1613*)

(LEONARD DIGGES *is speaking*)

Yes, so I said: 'twas labored "Cataline"
Insufferable for learning, tedious.
And so I said: the audience was kept
There at the Globe twelve years ago to hear:
"It is no matter; let no images
Be hung with Cæsar's trophies."

                  And to-day
They played his Julius Cæsar at the Court.
I saw it at the Globe twelve years ago,
A gala day! The flag over the Theatre
Fluttered the April breeze and I was thrilled.
And look what wherries crossed the Thames with freight
Of hearts expectant for the theatre.
For all the town was posted with the news
Of Shakespeare's "Julius Cæsar." So we paid
Our six-pence, entered, all the house was full.
And dignitaries, favored ones had seats
Behind the curtain on the stage. At last
The trumpet blares, the curtains part, Marullus

[17]

And Flavius enter, scold the idiot mob
And we sat ravished, listening to the close.

We knew he pondered manuscripts, forever
Was busy with his work, no rest, no pause.
Often I saw him leave the theatre
And cross the Thames where in a little room
He opened up his Plutarch. What was that?
A fertilizing sun, a morning light
Of bursting April! What was he? The earth
That under such a sun put forth and grew,
Showed all his valleys, mountain peaks and fields,
Brought forth the forests of his cosmic soul,
The coppice, jungle, blossoms good and bad.
A world of growth, creation! This the work,
Precedent force of Thomas North, his work
In causal link the Bishop of Auxerre,
And so it goes.

But others tried their hand
At Julius Cæsar, witness "Cæsar's Fall"
Which Drayton, Webster, others wrote. And look
At Jonson's "Cataline," that labored thing,
Dug out of Plutarch, Cicero. Go read,
Then read this play of Shakespeare's.

I recall
What came to me to see this, scene by scene,
Unroll beneath my eyes. 'Twas like a scroll

AT THE MERMAID TAVERN

Lettered in gold and purple where one theme
In firmest sequence, precious artistry
Is charactered, and all the sound and sense,
And every clause and strophe ministers
To one perfection. So it was we sat
Until the scroll lay open at our feet:
"According to his virtue, let us use him
With all respect and rites of burial,"
Then gasped for breath! The play's a miracle!
This world has had one Cæsar and one Shakespeare,
And with their birth is shrunk, can only bear
Less vital spirits.

                    For what did he do
There in that room with Plutarch? First his mind
Was ready with the very moulds of nature.
And then his spirit blazing like the sun
Smelted the gold from Plutarch, till it flowed
Molten and dazzling in these moulds of his.
And lo! he sets up figures for our view
That blind the understanding till you close
Eyes to reflect, and by their closing see
What has been done. O, well I could go on
And show how Jonson makes homonculus,
And Shakespeare gets with child, conceives and bears
Beauty of flesh and blood. Or I could say
Jonson lays scholar's hands upon a trait,
Ambition, let us say, as if a man
Were peak and nothing else thrust to the sky

AT THE MERMAID TAVERN

By blasting fires of earth, just peak alone,
No slopes, no valleys, pines, or sunny brooks,
No rivers winding at the base, no fields,
No songsters, foxes, nothing but the peak.
But Shakespeare shows the field-mice and the cricket,
The louse upon the leaf, all things that live
In every mountain which his soaring light
Takes cognizance; by which I mean to say
Shows not ambition only, that's the peak,
But mice-moods, cricket passions in the man;
How he can sing, or whine, or growl, or hiss,
Be bird, fox, wolf, be eagle or be snake.
And so this "Julius Cæsar" paints the mob
That stinks and howls, a woman in complaint
Most feminine shut from her husband's secrets;
Paints envy, paints the demagogue, in brief,
Paints Cæsar till we lose respect for Cæsar.
For there he stands in verity, it seems,
A tyrant, coward, braggart, aging man,
A stale voluptuary shoved about
And stabbed most righteously by patriots
To avenge the fall of Rome!

           Now I have said
Enough to give me warrant to say this:
This play of Shakespeare fails, is an abuse
Upon the memory of the greatest man
That ever trod this earth. And Shakespeare failed
By just so much as he might have achieved

AT THE MERMAID TAVERN

Surpassing triumph had he made the play
Cæsar instead of Brutus, had he shown
A sovereign will and genius struck to earth
With loss irreparable to Time and ruin
To Cæsar's dreams; struck evilly to death
By a mad enthusiast, a brutal stoic,
In whom all gratitude was tricked aside
By just a word, the word of Liberty.
Or might I also say the man had envy
Of Cæsar's greatness, or might it be true
Brutus took edge for hatred with the thought
That Brutus' sister flamed with love for Cæsar?
But who was Brutus, by the largest word
That comes to us that he should be exalted,
Forefronted in this play, and warrant given
To madmen down the ages to repeat
This act of Brutus', con the golden words
Of Shakespeare as he puts them in his mouth:
"Not that I loved him less, but loved Rome more.
He was ambitious so I slew him. Tears
For his love, joy for his fortune, honor for valor,
Death for ambition. Would you die all slaves
That Cæsar might still live, or live free men
With Cæsar dead?"

          And so it is the echo
Of Cæsar's fall is cried to by this voice
Of Shakespeare's and increased, to travel forth,
To fool the ages and to madden men

AT THE MERMAID TAVERN

With thunder in the hills of time to deeds
As horrible as this.

              Did Shakespeare know
The worth of Cæsar, that we may impute
Fault for this cartoon—caricature? Why look,
Did he not write the "mightiest Julius," write
"The foremost man of all the world," "the conqueror
Whom death could conquer not," make Cleopatra,
The pearl of all the east, say she was glad
That Cæsar wore her on his hand? He knew
What Cæsar's greatness was! Yet what have we?
A Cæsar with the falling sickness, deaf,
Who faints upon the offering of the crown;
Who envies Cassius stronger arms in swimming,
When it is known that Cæsar swam the Tiber,
Being more than fifty; pompous, superstitious,
Boasting his will, but flagging in the act;
Greedy of praise, incautious, unalert
To dangers seen of all; a lust incarnate
Of power and rulership; a Cæsar smashing
A great republic like a criminal,
A republic which had lived except for him.

So what was Rome when Cæsar took control?
All wealth and power concentered in the few;
A coterie of the rich who lived in splendor;
A working class that lived on doles of corn
And hordes of slaves from Asia, Africa,

AT THE MERMAID TAVERN

Who plotted murders in the dark purlieus;
The provinces were drained to feed the rich;
The city ruled by bribery, and corruption;
Armed gladiators sold their services.
And battled in the Forum; magistrates
Were freely scoffed at, consuls were attacked;
And orators spat in each other's faces
When reason failed them speaking in the Forum;
No man of prominence went on the streets
Without his hired gladiators, slaves.
The streets were unpoliced, no fire brigade,
Safe-guarded property. Domestic life
Was rotten at the heart, and vice was taught.
Divorce was rife and even holy Cato
Put by his wife.

          And this was the republic
That Cæsar took; and not the lovely state
Ordered and prospered, which ambitious Cæsar,
As Shakespeare paints him, over-whelmed. For Cæsar
Could execute the vision that the people
Deserve not what they want, but otherwise
What they should want, and in that mind was king
And emperor.

          And what was here for Shakespeare
To love and manifest by art, who hated
The Puritan, the mob? Colossus Cæsar,
Whose harmony of mind took deep offense

AT THE MERMAID TAVERN

At ugliness, disharmony! See the man:
Of body perfect and of rugged health,
Of graceful carriage, fashion, bold of eye,
A swordsman, horseman, and a general
Not less than Alexander; orator
Who rivalled Cicero, a man of charm,
Of wit and humor, versed in books as well;
Who at one time could dictate, read and write,
Composing grammars as he rode to war,
Amid distractions, dangers, battles, writing
Great commentaries. Yes, he is the man
In whom was mixed the elements that Nature
Might say:—this was a man—and not this Brutus.

Look at his camp, wherever pitched in Gaul,
Thronged by young poets, thinkers, scholars, wits,
And headed by this Cæsar, who when arms
Are resting from the battle, makes reports
Of all that's said and done to Cicero.
Here is a man large minded and sincere,
Active, a lover, conscious of his place,
Knowing his power, no reverence for the past,
Save what the past deserved, who made the task
What could be done and did it—seized the power
Of rulership and did not put it by
As Shakespeare clothes him with pretence of doing.
For what was kingship to him? empty name!
He who had mastered Asia, Africa,
Egypt, Hispania, after twenty years

[24]

AT THE MERMAID TAVERN

Of cyclic dreams and labor—king indeed!
A name! when sovereign power was nothing new.
He's fifty-six, and knows the human breed,
Sees man as body hiding a canal
For passing food along, a little brain
That watches, loves, attends the said canal.
He's been imperator at least two years—
King in good sooth! He knows he is not valued,
That he's misprized and hated, is compelled
To use whom he distrusts, despises too.
Why, what was life to him with such contempt
Of all this dirty world, this eagle set
Amid a flock of vultures, cow-birds, bats?
His ladder was not lowliness, but genius.
Read of his capture in Bithynia,
When he was just a stripling by Cilician
Pirates whom he treated like his slaves,
And told them to their face when he was ransomed
He'd have them crucified. He did it, too.
His ransom came at last, he was released,
And set to work at once to keep his word;
Fitted some ships out, captured every one
And crucified them all at Pergamos.
Not lowliness his ladder, but the strength
That.steps on shoulders, fit for steps alone.
So on this top-most rung he did not scan
The base degrees by which he did ascend,
But sickened rather at a world whose heights
Are not worth reaching. So it was he went

[25]

AT THE MERMAID TAVERN

Unarmed and unprotected to the Senate,
Knowing that death is noble, being nature,
And scorning fear. Why, he had lived enough.
The night before he dined with Lepidus,
To whom he said the death that is not seen,
Is not expected, is the best. But look,
Here in this play he's shown a weak old man,
Propped up with stays and royal robes, to amble,
Trembling and babbling to his coronation;
And to the going, driven by the fear
That he would be thought coward if he failed.
Who was to think so? Cassius, whom he cowed,
And whipped against strong odds, this Brutus, too,
There at Pharsalus! Faith, I'd like to know
What Francis Bacon thinks of this.

                          My friend,
Seeing the Rome that Cæsar took, we turn
To what he did with what he took. This Rome
At Cæsar's birth was governed by the people
In name alone, in fact the Senate ruled,
And money ruled the Senate. Rank and file
Was made of peasants, tradesmen, manumitted
Slaves and soldiers—these the populares,
Who made our Cæsar's uncle Marius
Chief magistrate six times. This was the party
That Cæsar joined and wrought for to the last.
He fought the aristocracy all his life.
His heart was democratic and his head

AT THE MERMAID TAVERN

Patrician—was ambitious from the first,
As Shakespeare is ambitious, gifted by
The Muses, must work out his vision or
Rot down with gifts neglected; so this Cæsar
Gifted to rule must rule—but what's the dream?
To use his power for democratic weal,
Bring order, justice in a rotten state,
And carry on the work of Marius,
His democratic uncle. Now behold,
He's fifty when he reaches sovereign power;
Few years are left in which he may achieve
His democratic ideas, for he sought
No gain in power, but chance to do his work,
Fulfill his genius. Well, he takes the Senate
And breaks its aristocracy, then frees
The groaning debtors; reduces the congestion
Of stifled Italy, founds colonies,
Helps agriculture, executes the laws.
Crime skulks before him, luxury he checks.
The franchise is enlarged, he codifies
The Roman laws, and founds a money system;
Collects a library, and takes a census;
Reforms the calendar, and thus bestrode
The world with work accomplished. Round his legs
All other men must peer; and envy, hatred
Were serpents at his heels, whose poison reached
His heart at last. He was the tower of Pharos,
That lighted all the world.

[27]

AT THE MERMAID TAVERN

                Now who was Brutus?
Cæsar forgave this Brutus seven times seven,
Forgave him for Pharsalia, all his acts
Of constant opposition. Who was Brutus?
A simple, honest soul? A heart of hate,
Bred by his uncle Cato! Was he gentle?
Look what he did to Salamis! Besieged
Its senate house and starved the senators
To force compliance with a loan to them
At 48 per cent! This is the man
Whom Shakespeare makes to say he'd rather be
A villager than to report himself
A son of Rome under these hard conditions,
Which Cæsar wrought! Who thought or called them
      hard?
Brutus or Shakespeare? Is it Plutarch, maybe,
Whom Shakespeare follows, all against the grain
Of truth so long revealed?
                 Do you not see
Matter in plenty for our Shakespeare's hand,
To show a sovereign genius and its work
Pursued by mad-dogs, bitten to its death,
Its plans thrown into chaos? Is there clay
Wherewith to mould the face of Cæsar; take
What clay remains to mould the face of Brutus?
Do you not see a straining of the stuff,
Making that big and salient which should be
Little and hidden in a group of figures?
And why, I ask? Here is the irony:

AT THE MERMAID TAVERN

Shakespeare has minted Plutarch, stamped the coin
With the face of Brutus. It's his inner genius,
The very flavor of his genius' flesh
To do this thing. Here is a world that's mad,
A Cæsar mad with power, a Brutus madder,
Being a dreamer, student, patriot
Who can't see things as clearly as the madman
Cæsar sees them, Brutus sees through books.
A mad-man butchered by a man more mad.
His father mad before him. Why, it's true
That every one is mad, because the world
Cannot be solved. Why are we here and why
This agony of being? Why these tasks
Imposed upon us never done, which drive
Our souls to desperation. So to print
The tragedy of life, our Shakespeare takes,
And by the taking shows he deems the theme
Greater than Cæsar's greatness: human will,
A dream, a hope, a love, and makes them big.
Strains all the clay to that around a form
Too weak to hold the moulded stuff in place.
Thus from his genius fashioning the tales
Of human life he passes judgment on
The mystery of life. Which could he do
By making Cæsar great, and would it be
So bitter and so hopeless if he did,
So adequate to curse this life of ours?
Why make a man as great as Nature can
The gods will raise a manakin to kill him,

And over-turn the order that he founds.
A grape seed strangles Sophocles, a turtle
Falls from an eagle's claws on Aeschylos,
And cracks his shiny pate.

                So at the last
The question is, is history the truth,
Or is the Shakespeare genius, which arranges
History to speak the Shakespeare mood,
Reaction to our life, the truth?

                And here
I leave you to reflect. Let's one more ale
And then I go.

CHARLOTTE CORDAY

(The Revolutionary Tribunal; July 17th, 1793)

MONTANÉ, *Presiding judge.*
FOUQUIER-TINVILLE, *Prosecutor.*
CHAVEAU-LAGARDE, *Defending counsel.*
DANTON, ⎱
ROBESPIERRE, ⎰ *Leaders of the Jacobins.*
MADAM EVARD, *Marat's friend.*
CHARLOTTE CORDAY.

MONTANÉ
Where is your home?

CHARLOTTE
Caen.

MONTANÉ
Why did you come to Paris?

CHARLOTTE
To kill Marat.

MONTANÉ
Why?

[31]

CHARLOTTE CORDAY

CHARLOTTE
His crimes.

MONTANÉ
What crimes?

CHARLOTTE
The woes of France! His readiness to fire
All France with civil war.

MONTANÉ
You meant to kill
When you struck?

CHARLOTTE
Yes! I meant to kill.

MONTANÉ
How old are you?

CHARLOTTE
Twenty-four.

MONTANÉ
A woman
Young as you are could not have done this murder
Unless abetted.

CHARLOTTE
No! You little know
The human heart. The hatred of one's heart
Impels the hand better than other's hate.

[32]

CHARLOTTE CORDAY

MONTANÉ
You hated Marat?

CHARLOTTE
                    Hated! I did not kill
A man, I killed a wild beast eating up
The people and the nation.

FOUQUER-TINVILLE
                    She's familiar
With crime, no doubt.

CHARLOTTE
                    You monster! Do you take me
For just a common murderer?

FOUQUER-TINVILLE
                         Yes! Why not?
Here is your knife!

CHARLOTTE
                    Oh! Yes, I recognize it.
I bought it at the cutler's shop.

MONTANÉ
                    What for?

CHARLOTTE
To kill Marat with; cost me forty sous.
After I came to Paris—

[33]

CHARLOTTE CORDAY

FOUQUER-TINVILLE
     When?

CHARLOTTE
          Four days ago.

FOUQUER-TINVILLE
That was the day you wrote Marat?

CHARLOTTE
          Same day.

FOUQUER-TINVILLE
Saying you knew of news in Caen, knew
Means by the which Marat could render service
To the Republic!

CHARLOTTE
          By his death!

FOUQUER-TINVILLE
              But yet
You gave him credit in this note for love
Of France, our France. You tricked him.

CHARLOTTE
          Like a viper.
He was a mad-dog, dog-leech, alley rat,
With bits of carrion festering 'twixt his teeth,

[34]

CHARLOTTE CORDAY

Hair glued with ordure, urine. Why not trick
By best means, so to catch a beast with fangs
As venomous as his? He was a fire
That crawled and licked its way; why not put out
The fire by water, snuffing, stamping, why
Be precious of the means?

MADAM EVARD

You know me, woman?

CHARLOTTE

You struck me when I stabbed him. You're his whore!

MADAM EVARD

Oh! Oh!

ROBESPIERRE

(*To Danton*)

This is enough! When fury claws at fury.
I hear the tumbril for her. Come!

DANTON

The slut!

(*Danton and Robespierre leave the room together.*)

CHARLOTTE

Was that not Robespierre who left the room?

FOUQUER-TINVILLE

Why do you ask?

[35]

CHARLOTTE CORDAY

CHARLOTTE

I wanted him for counsel.

FOUQUER-TINVILLE

For what? The guillotine?

CHARLOTTE

(*Shrinking*)   You monster! You!

MONTANÉ

Have you a lawyer?

CHARLOTTE

No! I wrote Doulcet.
He shirks the honor, doubtless; have not heard.
I thought of Chabot and of Robespierre.

MONTANÉ

Chauveau-Lagarde shall counsel you. Proceed!

FOUQUER-TINVILLE

Is this your letter?

CHARLOTTE

Yes.

FOUQUER-TINVILLE

This letter here
Is written to a man named Barbarous,
Her lover—

CHARLOTTE CORDAY

CHARLOTTE

No! You monster!

FOUQUER-TINVILLE

Very well!
Is this yours: "To the French, friends of the laws,
And friends of peace."

CHARLOTTE

Yes! I admit what's true.

FOUQUER-TINVILLE

And is this yours: "To the Committee of Public Safety"?

CHARLOTTE

I wrote it, yes.

FOUQUER-TINVILLE

Let's see now what's her mind.
This letter to the friends of peace and laws:—
"O France, thy peace depends upon the laws."
Laws! And she hastens to the cutler's shop,
And buys a knife with which to slay Marat.
Now look! This friend of France's peace and laws
Must dodge self-contradiction. How? That's plain:
"I do not break the law, killing Marat."
Why? What's Marat? A man? Of course, a man.
But then an "out-law," as she writes. How's that?
Outlawed by whom? Charlotte Corday of Caen!
What else? A man! But then condemned. By whom?
"The universe." Voila! The universe

[37]

CHARLOTTE CORDAY

Is swallowed by her swollen vanity.
She speaks for God, for solar systems, stars;
Adjudges laws, interprets, executes;
Is greater than the Revolution, France.
She's a descendant of the great Corneille;
A stage imagination, actress, acts,
And quotes here in this letter from Voltaire's
"Mort de César." Now listen what her hate
Has used for whetrock, in the words of Brutus:
"Whether the world astonished loads my name
"And deed with horror, admiration, censure,
"I do not care, nor care to live in Time.
"I act indifferent to reproach or glory,
"A free, untrameled patriot am I.
"Duty accomplished I shall rest content.
"Think only, friends, how you may break your chains."
So Brutus lives in her! And like disease
Loosed from the crumbling cerements and dust
Of broken tombs, the madness which slew Cæsar
Infects, makes mad this woman; and she slays
The great Marat!
                    She does not care for the world's
Censure or admiration! Does not care
To live in time! She lies! Why, in this room
A man, Huer, is sketching her. Behold
He's drawing now her face for Time to see.
And in this letter written to the Committee
She says: *"Since I have little time to live,*
"I trust you will permit me to have painted

CHARLOTTE CORDAY

"My portrait." Why? If careless if she live
In memory or time? The secret's out,
And written in her hand: *"I want to leave*
"A picture for remembrance to my friends."
What friends? Her father? Barbarous? Caen,
Paris, the whole of France, the world, if Time
Writes down the people's friend as beast, would see
The face, in such case, which destroyed Marat,
Condemned first by the "universe" and at last
By France, the world! What next? She doubts her
　　God,
Her Brutus warrant, "universe" approval,
And writes here as a reason, in addition:
"That as men cherish memory of good men,
"So curiosity"—see her spirit flop
And smile with idiot guilt upon itself—
"So curiosity sometimes seeks out
"Memorials of criminals." That's her word:
"Criminals," and by that word she stands
Self-dedicated to the guillotine.

Charlotte

Well, am I not a criminal in the eyes
Of such a beast as you? Will nature spawn
No other beasts like you?

Fouquer-Tinville

　　　　　　　　Yes, in my eyes,
You are a criminal. But you mistake.

[39]

CHARLOTTE CORDAY

I have no curiosity about you.
When you are dead I'd have your name erased,
Your face erased, lest it corrupt the face
Of Brutus, and lead hands in years to come
To speak the "universe," interpret "laws,"
And slay whom they would slay.

                              This is not all
About her picture, a memorial
For admiration by posterity.
She writes this Barbarous, lover or what,
It matters nothing, writes him pages here
In detail of herself, and intimate
Portrayal of her feelings: how she planned,
And killed Marat.   To Barbarous she writes
About her letter to the Committee, asking
To have her portrait painted.   *Now,* for whom?
Her friends?   Not now!   For the department now
Of Calvados.   There! hanging on a wall,
A prize of history, is the deathless face
Of Charlotte Corday, destroyer of Marat,
Saviour of France, as *Brutus struck for Rome!*
Yes, I invite your thought to what she writes
To Barbarous: description of her act
In sneaking to Marat with hidden knife;
And as he sat there helpless in the tub,
And unsuspecting of her hatred, quick
She rips him like a butcher.   Then, "A moi!"
He cries, "A moi!"   And she's elate, her eyes

CHARLOTTE CORDAY

Bright as the lightning that has struck. Look now!
How she writhes here, how passing cross her face
Are lights of ghastly fields of fire and clouds
When hurricanes descend.

CHARLOTTE
You beast! You beast!

FOUQUER-TINVILLE
I am a beast, eh? *You* are what? I'll tell.
From Caen, as 'tis known. She's being sketched,
I'll sketch her too. You see, she's strongly built,
Large eyes of blue, large features, handsome though;
Nose shapely, and good teeth; equipped to play
In dramas of Corneille, her ancestor.
She needs a man. A husband would have drawn
Innocuously the electric passion, which
Collected in a bolt to loose and lurch
Against Marat. All women should be farmed.
She has her schooling in a convent, reads;
Lives with her thoughts and dreams. I'll sketch her soul:
Has not enough of living to consume
The forces of her dreams. She reads Rousseau,
And Plutarch's heroes, Brutus most of all.
Thrills at the words "Republic," "Liberty."
Thinks the Girondists only can set up
A real republic. Ideas are the stuff
Of history. Kill ideas or be killed
By ideas is the fate of man. Republic,

[41]

CHARLOTTE CORDAY

Liberty, Brutus are ideas. Ideas
Are dangerous, being truths, more so as lies.
And lies destroyed Marat.

                              Who was Marat?
A man of study, learning. Physicist,
Admired of Franklin, Göethe for his works
On heat and light; a doctor, having won
An honorary title at St. Andrew's
In England. Linguist, speaking Spanish, German,
Italian, English. Versed in Governments:—
You know his work on England's constitution
Whereby he sought to clear the mind of France—
This Charlotte Corday's with the rest—that England
Is free, her systems free; stop the Girondists
From that re-iterated lie; stop France
From taking on the English system.

                                    So
True ideas of Marat, evolved from life,
Living and study must combat, destroy
False ideas of Girondists, will succeed;
But cannot bar the door to the idea
That enters at his bathroom with a knife.
How was it that no valet and no guard
Preserved him? Why? Lovers of liberty
Starve in her service!

                            But there was a time
When he knew elegance and privacy.

But Liberty and Wisdom would be served.
He went to rags, was hunted, had to hide
In sewers for the cause of Liberty;
And there took loathsome trouble, eased at times
By steam, hot tubs. And thus our people's friend
Is found accessible to this female lie,
Girondist lie, possessing her, and stabbed.
Or at the best ideas of Liberty
Conduct her to his bath-room, where Marat
Is tubbed in sequence and in punishment
Of his idea of Liberty. Gods can laugh,
But men must weep. O worthless, rotten world!
It is most pitiful, most tragic, lifts
Man's heart to spit at heaven, that these friends
Of peoples must be slain, starved, hunted first,
Then butchered for their service and their love.
Saved not by truth; destroyed by lies, a lie
That he was evil, by the maniac lie
Of her mad vision that she knew what Freedom,
Liberty, Republic mean. Slain by the lie
Of this Girondist dream, this milk and water,
Emasculated, luke-warm craft of states:
Girondists: patches on the robes of kings;
Girondists: autogamists; mating sisters,
The past, and in the mating without child
Of truth or progress. Neither hot nor cold,
Spewed, therefore, from the mouth of Time. Betrayers,
Waylayers of the brave, the clear of eye;
Girondists: 'twixt republicans and kings,

And holding hands of each to make them friends.
Workers and owners of the new foaled mule
Bred of the royal stallion and an ass.
Girondists! loving wealth and ease, the church
Which loves them too. Girondists picking steps
Of moderate reform. Girondists hating
The Revolution, which must kill the foes
Of Liberty, as criminals are killed
For robbery, yet rejoice to see the blood
Of dead Marat. They're lofty! They are pure!
They love the laws, love peace! Yes, as this woman
Loves law and peace.

                What is it like? A play
Where all is mimicked. Do we talk of facts?
Are these not fautocinni? Where's the hand
That plays this coarse and bloody joke to eyes
Of men that crave reality? I mean this:
A woman with lovers who suggest, abet;
A woman with no man, who dreams and reads,
Lives in the stench of these Girondist lies;
Ghosts float on fogs of her miasmic soul.
She hears Marat's a monster, dabbling blood,
A rabid ignoramus running foul
Of liberty and order, nihilist,
And sanguinary madman, dragon slimed
In back-wash of all hatred, envy, lust
Of the dispossessed, malformed, misborn; and then
She dreams of Brutus, who struck down—there now

[44]

CHARLOTTE CORDAY

I nail a lie that will be always truth
To Charlotte Cordays.   Cæsar!   Tyrant?   **No.**
No man is tyrant who sees truth and rules
For truth's sake.   For the ruled must share the truth
Where Cæsars rule.

                    So much for her.   She stands
Watchful and envious in the wings, and sees
Marat, not as we see him; not as Time
Will see Marat.   L'Ami du Peuple to her
Is enemy of France, of Liberty.
This man most rare, most pure of soul, most clear
Of vision that the contest lies between
The rich and poor, has always lain between
The rich and poor, and not between the people
And kings; that poverty's the thing, is seen
By Charlotte Corday from the wings, as nothing
But hatred, murder.

               Well, my girl, you'll get
Your picture in the galleries of history.
You'll get it; and to choke you with your words:
"So curiosity would have memorials
"Of criminals, which serve to keep alive
"Horror for their crimes."

                 Your picture's up
Already.   Horror stares!   You killed Marat.
That is your place in Time: you killed Marat!

CHARLOTTE CORDAY

You sneaked upon a great man, true man, weak
From torture of disease, contracted serving
Democracy, and slew him like a beast.
Charlotte Corday, assassin! That's your place,
And character in history.

CHARLOTTE
                                    Let it be.
Assassin. Well, assassins kill assassins:
The words repel, destroy each other, sir.
If any grieve for me I beg of them
To think of me in the Elysian Fields
With Brutus and the heroes.

CHAVEAU-LAGARDE
                                    Gentlemen!
The deed's admitted. What to say, but ask
Your clemency? The girl's fanatical.
The prosecutor argues well for me
In saying that a lie corrupted her,
And maddened her to act; which is to say
If that lie were a truth, she had the right
To slay Marat. With this regard Voltaire,
Great minds before him, painted Brutus great
Because he slew a tyrant. But if Cæsar
Was not a tyrant, how does Brutus stand
But mad-man who believed, was honest, slew
In honesty of heart? Then what's the case?
To punish for ill-judging of the facts,

[46]

CHARLOTTE CORDAY

Or mercy show for human frailty
Of judgment and of vision? Great Marat
Has done his work, and left his legacy.
We cannot help him, meting death for death.
And would his noble spirit ask her death?
Think of it! You will answer no, I think.
He would say: kill the ideas of Caen,
The world which fires these Charlottes with a lie.
Smallpox is deadly as a butcher knife,
He had to die. The syllabus is death
In this our human logic: what's the odds
What premises produce conclusions? Knives,
Consumptions, fevers, wars? We may be gods
Withholding death where we have power to kill;
Withhold it saying: She mistook, believed
A lie, was faultless for believing it,
And slew believing. Were it truth and all
Believed we would applaud, as nations war,
Bound in a common vision of one truth.
The Revolution, France, will lose not, rather
Gain by this clemency; 'twill lift a light,
First in the world, of reason, justice purged
Of hatred's refuse: vengeance, fear, all passions
Of bitterness of soul. We worship Reason,
And this is Reason.

CHARLOTTE
                    You have done your part
And served me well. I thank you.

CHARLOTTE CORDAY

The Jury

Let her join
Brutus in the Elysian Fields. We say:
The guillotine!

The Mob

(*Outside*)   To the guillotine!   To the guillotine!

Charlotte

I am content.

A MAN CHILD IS BORN

(February 12th, 1809. Log Hut near Hodgenville, Ky.)

(A neighbor woman is talking)

The wind blows through the chinks—it's snowing too,
Tom piles the logs on, but that door is loose.
An earthen floor is always cold. You're warm.
I'm glad I brought a kiverlid along,
An extra one comes handy at this time.
You are all right—you had an easy time,
Considering this baby, big and long.
He's very long, will be a tall man, too,
A hunter and a chopper, Indian fighter,
Lord, who knows what, a big man in the country,
A preacher, congressman or senator,
A president—who knows? God blesses you
To give you such a son. He nurses well.
Don't let him have too much at first. You see
That single window gives too little light
To show you what he's like. He looks a little
Like Nancy Shipley Hanks, your mother, perhaps
A little like your aunt, old Mary Lincoln.
Since you and Tom are cousins, it may be

[49]

A MAN CHILD IS BORN

This boy will be a mixture, but if folks
Resemble animals, the traits of you
Will be made stronger in this child, because
You two are cousins.

                        You will be up to see
What he looks like, in just a week or so.
Perhaps when next the flames mount in the fire-place
The light will show you.   Have you named him yet—
Tom likes the name of Abraham—well, that's good—
You've chosen that!

                       I thought I heard a step—
Who do you think is coming?   Dennis Hanks!
He's come to see his cousin Abraham.

Good mornin', Dennis! come into the fire—
I'll let you see your cousin Abraham—
A big, long baby—quick! and shut the door,
The room is none too warm, the wind is blowing—
Tom's gone for logs again!   Here, I'll raise up
The kiverlid and let you see—look here!
You think he's homely!   Pretty is, you know,
As pretty does—but see how big and long!
In fifteen years he'll make you up and come
To beat him wrestling, I will bet a coon's skin.
Now you may kiss him; in a little bit
I'll let you hold him by the fire.   The pot
Is on for dinner, we are having squirrel

A MAN CHILD IS BORN

And hominy for dinner—you can stay.
Now clear out, Dennis—I must do some things—
Open the door for Tom, he's coming there
With logs to mend the fire!

RICHARD BOOTH TO HIS SON JUNIUS BRUTUS

(London, December 13th, 1813.)

So you're to play Campillo, all in spite
Of my commands, at Deptford?   Here's the bill
Found in your pocket.   You are seventeen,
Too young for this adventure in the world.
What will you be, a strolling vagabond,
Smelling of grease, impoverished, set apart
From stable folk by this, your wandering art?
And just to think I named you Junius Brutus,
After the great republican who slew
The Roman tyrant Cæsar—I myself
A worshipper of Liberty all my life,
And choosing such a patronym for you
To dedicate you to the faith in me.
Now you would leave this dignity to speak
Mimetic words, and act.   I beg of you,
Listen, my boy, before it is too late,
And let me tell my story to you now,
That you may profit by the things I've lived. . . .

You see that face of Washington, hung up
There on the wall where every entering eye

RICHARD BOOTH TO HIS SON

Must mark it? You remember that I ask,
Enforce respect to Washington and make
The passer bow his head—well, listen now:

It's seventeen seventy-seven, I'm fourteen.
Burgoyne's surrender fires my tender heart.
We hear Lord George Germain forgets to take
A letter from a pigeon hole containing
Instructions to Burgoyne that touches on
The campaign on the Hudson. Anyway,
Burgoyne gets tangled in the wilderness
Around Champlain. He faces broken bridges,
And trees felled in his way. His horses fail,
Provisions are exhausted. Then he sends
A thousand men to Bennington to get
More horses and provisions. There he's stumped:
A veteran of Bunker Hill is there,
A Colonel Stark, whose wife is Mollie Stark,
Who says we beat the British here to-day,
Or Mollie Stark's a widow. August 16th
They whipped the British soundly—and Burgoyne
Was driven to defeat.

                         That made us flame!
I was a hot republican. Slipped away
To Paris with a cousin to set sail
For America and help the Americans,
And wrote from there a letter to John Wilkes,
And asked his help to get me in the army

[53]

RICHARD BOOTH TO HIS SON

Of Washington. As Englishmen, I wrote,
It may be said we are not justified
In taking arms against the English cause.
That argument with you could have no weight,
You, who have fought for Liberty so long.
And England, what is she? All human rights
Are lost in England under tyrant rule.
It is the duty of an English heart
To help those whom this lawless tyranny
Oppresses in America. So I wrote,
And sent to London. What do you suppose?
John Wilkes went to my father with this letter.
They caught me, brought me home, and here I am,
A lawyer to this day. You think it strange!
Who was John Wilkes, that he should thus betray?—
I wonder, even now.

       For he had been
A rebel spirit from his boyhood up,
Born here in London seventeen twenty-seven;
Was sent to Parliament when he was thirty.
Attacked the king in writing, was arrested;
Refused to answer questions, then they chucked
Our rebel in the Tower; he got out,
Saying he had a privilege as a member
Of Parliament. They passed a special law
To warrant prosecution, ousted him
From Parliament, and then he went to France,
Was outlawed, but returned, again was sent

RICHARD BOOTH TO HIS SON

To Parliament, before he took his seat.
Was sent to prison on the sentences
Passed on the old conviction, and expelled
From Parliament again for libeling
The minister of war.   Three times again
They elected him to Parliament, but they kept
Our rebel out.   He now became the people's
Idol for his sufferings and his courage.
They let him out of prison, made him mayor
Of London, and in seventeen seventy-four
He goes from Middlesex to Parliament
And takes his seat at last, and there he was
When I wrote to him, seventeen seventy seven.
Why did he tell my father, send my father
The letter which I wrote?

                    I know, I think:
He knew the dangers, agonies ahead,
For a boy who sets his feet along the path
Of Liberty and working for the world
To free the world—and did not know my stuff;
Whether I had the will to fight and die
With no regrets.   He knew what he had suffered,
And had a tenderness for the youth who flames
And beats his wings for freedom, would release
From tyranny and wrong.

                    And so they caught me,
And brought me home and set me to the law.

RICHARD BOOTH TO HIS SON

And here I am, who never lost the dream
And named you Junius Brutus. Oh, my son,
Leave off this actor calling, stay with me,
I who was nipped would see you grow to flower,
Fulfill my vision. What, you promise me,
If I will let you act this time, to come
And let me mould you, teach you what I know,
Fill full your spirit with the hope I had,
That you may do what I have failed to do?
You promise that? Well, Junius Brutus, go
And may you fail at acting and return.

A MAN CHILD IS BORN

(July 14th, 1839.   The Farm.)

(Mrs. Booth is speaking.)

After such pain this child against my breast!
Oh what a cunning head and little face!
What coal black hair!   You have begun to feed!
Look, doctor, how he feeds—why look at him,
He is a little man!   Is not God good
To give me such a baby?   Well, I think
You will be something noble in this world,
And something great, you precious little man!
His daddy wants to name him John Wilkes.   I
Would name him Junius Brutus to hand down
His father's glory and perhaps his art.
Look, doctor, is it not a miracle
That God performs, this little life from mine,
This beauty out of love!   I pray to God
To bless you, little John, if that's your name.
A colored mammy read the coffee grounds,
And says he will be famous, rich and great—
He may be so.   I know he will be good.
Look at that darling face—it must be so!

[57]

SQUIRE BOWLING GREEN

(Rutledge's Tavern, New Salem, July 14th, 1839.)

You missed it—case all over! Lincoln's gone.
He's just had time about to reach the mill.
He couldn't wait until the stage arrived.
Had business in the courts of Springfield—well,
You can believe he has become a lawyer.
He borrowed Mentor Graham's horse to ride.
John Yoakum is in Springfield and to-morrow
Will bring it back.

               Who won the case? Why, Abe.
He won it by his horse-sense and his wit.
You must have met the jury down the road.
What were they laughing at? About the case.
We started yesterday on the evidence
And finished up this morning. An appeal?
The verdict satisfies both parties, and
My judgment stands.

              Abe is a natural lawyer,
Knows things that can't be found in books, although
He knows the books. And why not? You recall
When he was boarding with me how he studied?

SQUIRE BOWLING GREEN

It's just four years ago or so, that he
Came home one night with Blackstone. Well, I've
    noticed
A man attracts what's his, just like a magnet
Draws bits of steel.   You can't make me believe
That Blackstone came to him unless 'twas meant
That he should be a lawyer.   Don't you know?
He read this Blackstone in his store all day
And half the night as well.   He said to me
Not Volney's "Ruins," Shakespeare, Burns, had taken
His interest like this Blackstone.   Yes, he took it
When he went fishing with Jack Kelso, read,
And let Jack row the boat and bait the hooks. . . .

I think he knows this Blackstone all by heart.
But anyway, he knows the human heart.
Well, now here is the case: Here is a colt.
George Cameron says the colt is his—John Spears
Says no, the colt is mine, and Cameron sues,
And Spears defends, and sixty witnesses
Come here to testify, on my word it's true,
On my judicial oath it is the fact.
The thirty swear the colt is Cameron's;
And thirty swear the colt belongs to Spears;
And not a man impeached, these witnesses
Are everyone good men, and most of them
I know as I know you.   Well, what's to do?
The scales are balanced.   And besides all this,
Here's Cameron who swears the colt is his,

SQUIRE BOWLING GREEN

And Spears who swears the opposite, and both
Are credible, I know them both. So I
Sit like a fellow trying to decide
What happens when a thing impenetrable
Is struck by something irresistible—
I'm stumped, that's all.

          You see the facts were these:
Each of these fellows owns a mare, the mares
Look pretty much alike, each had a colt
In April. But the other day one colt—
Which colt, that is the question—strayed away
And can't be found. George Cameron has a colt—
These men are neighbors—but John Spears comes over
And sees the colt at Cameron's in the field;
And says, "That is my colt." "Not on your life,"
George Cameron replies, "The colt is mine—
Your colt has strayed, not mine." They come to law.
John Spears gets Lincoln, and they come to court
With sixty witnesses; and here this noon
With all the evidence put in, I sit
And eye the jury, know the jury's stumped,
As I am stumped.

          Then Lincoln says: "Your honor,
Let's have a trial on view." I'd heard of that,
But never sat on such a trial before.
"Let's bring the colt, the two mares over here,

SQUIRE BOWLING GREEN

And let the jury see which mare the colt
Resembles, let the jury use their eyes
As witnesses use theirs."

                      That seemed fair.
And so we sent one fellow for the mares,
Another for the colt.   For Lincoln said:
"Your honor, bring them separate, so the jury
Can have the sudden flash of seeing them
Separate, to study them."

                  For an hour
Abe sat here in the shade and told us stories.
And pretty soon we heard the horses whinney,
And heard the colt.   And Lincoln said, "Your honor,
Let's have the mares led past the jury, trotting,
Let's see their pace."   And so they trotted them.
"Now trot the colt," said Lincoln—we did that.
The jury watched to see the look of legs,
And movement, if you please, to catch a likeness.
But nothing came of this.   Then Lincoln said:
"Now turn the colt loose"—and they turned it loose.
It galloped to the mare of Spears and sucked!
Well, now it's true a colt's a silly thing,
And may mistake its mother, but a mare
Will never let a colt that's not her own
Put under flanks its nose.   Of course the jury,
And all of us know that—and so did Abe.

SQUIRE BOWLING GREEN

.The jury yelled and all the witnesses
Began to whoop. And when I rapped for order
And got things quiet—Lincoln rose and said,
"I rest, your honor."

              So I entered judgment
For Spears. They went to Berry's for the drinks—
There! hear them laughing.

                    Lincoln took his fee,
Ten dollars, I believe, and went to Springfield.

LINCOLN SPEAKING IN CONGRESS

(January 12th, 1848.)

"Any people anywhere being inclined and having the power have the right to rise up and shake off the existing government and form a new one that suits them better. This is a most valuable, a sacred right. A right which we hope and believe is to liberate the world. Nor is this right confined to cases in which the whole people of an existing government may choose to exercise it. Any portion of such people that can, may revolutionize, and may make their own of so much of the territory as they inhabit. More than this, a majority of any portion of such people may revolutionize, putting down a minority, intermingled with, or near about them, who may oppose their movement. Such minority was precisely the case of the Tories of our own revolution. It is a quality of revolutions not to go by old lines, or old laws, but to break up both and make new ones."

JOHN WILKES BOOTH AT THE FARM

(January 12th, 1848.)

Mother, I'm breathless! I have seen a man,
The strangest man I ever saw. I'm scared!
I went down to the hollow, was at play,
Was marching with my broomstick gun—and then
While I stood there and said "attention," playing
Soldier, you know, reciting to my soldiers,
I heard a voice—looked round and saw this man.
He was enormous with a frightful face,
Black eyes, black hair, a voice that sounded like
Low thunder, though it could be soft and sweet.
And he said to me, "What's your name, my boy?"
I told him. Then he said, "Where is your father?"
I said, "My father's gone." "Where is your mother?"
"Up at the house," I answered. Then he asked,
"What are you doing here?" "Why, playing soldier."
"Are you a patriot?" And I said yes.
"Oh, no," he said, "your father was an actor;
I saw him play the part of Brutus often,
And you will be an actor, you've the look."
How did he know these things, do you suppose?
And then he said, "Recite for me." "I can't,"
I said to him. "O yes, you can," he said.

[64]

JOHN WILKES BOOTH AT THE FARM

"You must recite for me."   And I was scared,
Began to cry, and he said, "Hush, my boy,
I will not hurt you, but you must recite,
I want to see what you have memorized."
So I was choking, but I tried to do it:
"The tyrannous and bloody deed is done,
The most arch act of piteous massacre
That ever yet this land was guilty of." . . .

"No Richard III," he said.   "Here look at me!
Why do you dodge?   Why not recite some words
From Brutus, for you know them, why, my boy?
You've heard your father speak the words of Brutus.
Why do you hide your knowledge?   Look at me!"
He terrified me so that I began:
"It must be by his death: and for my part
I know no personal cause to spurn at him,
But for the general.   He would be crowned:
How that might change his nature, there's the question.
It is the bright day that brings forth the adder."
I got so far and saw him looking down,
As if he saw—I don't know what—and then
I stopped and looked—and there I saw an adder
Coiled close to me. I jumped and screamed.   He
    laughed—
I ran away, and left him standing there.
Mother, I am afraid.   Who was this man?
My head hurts.   I'm afraid.   Keep close to me—
I am so frightened.

JUNIUS BRUTUS BOOTH

(On a steamboat bound for Cincinnati from New Orleans, November 30th, 1852.)

You are a doctor? Ill? I'm very ill.
My soul is worn, it is a ghastly life,
This acting, traveling, living through the passions
Of Brutus, and Orestes, Richard III.
My father tried to make a lawyer of me,
But fate is fate. My age is fifty-six,
But counting by the moments I have lived
A thousand years were nearer truth. Oh, well,
What if this talking tire me, I am tired
With such fatigue that nothing adds to it.
And if I die, why what will be, will be.
I'd like to see "The Farm" in Maryland
Just once again, see Mary, that's my wife,
John Wilkes, my boy, and Junius Brutus, too—
Edwin I left in California,
Shall never see him more I fear—but then
What comes to us must come.

                                    That brandy helps,
I'm better now.

[66]

JUNIUS BRUTUS BOOTH

Oh, yes, it's true my father
Would make a lawyer of me, couldn't do it—
I am a better lawyer than he was
For acting parts and living other lives,
Thus finding laws of life—but what's the good?
You can't find happiness, all is vanity.
If you're a strolling player, vanity;
Vexation too and jealousy and strife.
If all the house goes mad to see you rage
As life-like as the Moor did, do they know
What realest envy stalks behind the scenes,
What you have done to keep your golden voice,
Your strength to paint the frenzy of Othello?

After one greatest triumph I sat alone,
Was playing solitaire, who should come in?
Chief Justice Marshall, friend of mine? Oh, yes.
He said, "I think you'd be the happiest
Of men, why not enjoy what you've achieved?"
"Judge," I replied, "you see me here alone,
There is no ecstasy, no drop of joy
For me save in that moment when I see,
Both through my genius glowing and the cries
And plaudits from the house, that I have struck.
The fateful note that thrills—all other hours
Are spent in saving power and making ready
For just that moment. What's an actor, poet?
A medium round whom the spirits swarm
Like bats in Tartarus and shrill Me! Me!

[67]

JUNIUS BRUTUS BOOTH

Take now and write, speak for me—make it clear,
You are our hope of truth, of being known
For what we are.   And so you're never done.
The spirits dash about you with their cries;
Men note your eyes turned inward—move away.
And you must keep in vigor.   Hoarseness rasps
The voice of Brutus, you must catch no cold.
You drink sometimes to deafen ears against
The spirits' crying, but you pay for it,
Must climb back into strength, but while you're weak
The spirits are a-crying, there you are,
Ambitious but enfeebled, can't respond,
And tortured for it.   There is no escape.
And so you play at solitaire."
                              The Judge
Replied: "A judge is lonely, for his reasons
Must keep himself aloof."
                              Yes, I knew Kean.
He played Othello to my great Iago,
And I say great, for I was twenty-one,
And made the London English shout and howl:
"Great Booth forever," though they shouted, too,
"No Booth" and "down with Booth," the partisans
Of Kean, the envious.   And on a time
It's Drury Lane, and what an audience!
Hazlitt is there and Godwin, Shelley's friend,
John Howard Payne, who wrote "The Fall of Tarquin."
He saw that Kean was envious, would not be
Excelled by me and wrote as much.

JUNIUS BRUTUS BOOTH

My friend,
Another drink of brandy!

Well, at last
I make America my home. 'Twere well
If I am spared to write my memories,
They throng so at this moment. God be praised,
I knew Old Hickory and supped with him,
A man from top to toe! And I have lived,
Fought, suffered, triumphed, lived through self and lived
Through Brutus, Lear, and Richard.

Look at me,
Am I a man you'd ever take for mad?
Mad-men have struck at me, a lunatic
Struck at me with an ax, I cowed his hate
And fixed him with my eye. But as for me,
Here have I been for life a lover of home,
A husband blest with happiness in a wife,
And yet reputed mad. For little things
Like this reputed mad: I'm playing Shylock,
The call boy searches me, my time has come,
Where was I? In a closet. Was it queer?
A symptom? No! I hid to shut the light
Of other things external from the mind
Of Shylock's mood. Why, is it strange at all
For a soul that incarnates itself with souls
Like Brutus' and Lear's to lose itself,
Seem sometimes naked, trembling, swaying too
With such exhaustion, such tremendous change?

[69]

JUNIUS BRUTUS BOOTH

These common minds see not the genius mind
For what it is, forget the strength and wisdom
That makes the genius, in my case, forget
My books and scholarship, my toil, who learned
Greek, Latin, German, French and Arabic,
Hebrew and Spanish; the philosophies,
I've mastered in my life.

                                        I tremble too
For thinking of my little son, John Wilkes,
So beautiful and gifted, has the touch;
Is full of dreams, goes charging on his horse,
Spouting heroic speeches, lance in hand
There on "The Farm," a patriot and a lover
Of liberty even now. What will he be,
A statesman or an actor, warrior, what?
God knows alone, and what his fate God knows.
I named him after John Wilkes, patriot
And English libertarian—but no matter,
He'll do what he will do. They named me Brutus
And I became an actor, not a statesman,
Warrior, no tyrannicide.

                        Hold there!
What is this? Take my hand! Sharp pain again—
Pray! pray! pray!

                    (*He dies.*)

A CERTAIN POET ON THE DEBATES

(At Alton, Illinois, October 15th, 1858.)
(Arguing with a group at the hotel.)

Why do I speak with such authority?
I know this matter through from A to Z;
I know it just as well as Lincoln knows it.
There's not a document I have not studied
From Elliott's Debates to this Le Compton
Kansas constitution that has escaped
My mind's analysis. And you will see
Lincoln is beaten now. You are absurd
To think he'll win the presidency for losing
The senatorship—clean crazy all of you!

Who am I? Well, it makes no difference.
I am a mind, a mere intelligence
Going about this year of fifty-eight
An observer and a listener. Gabriel
Could be no more impersonal than I.
I've followed up these fellows like the boy
That trails the circus, clear from Ottawa
To Freeport, Charleston, Galesburg, Quincy, Alton;
And made my way at first with sawing wood,
Later by selling razors, soap and strops;

[71]

A CERTAIN POET ON THE DEBATES

And just to hear the speaking, see the crowds—
These crowds that leave the shop and farms, these crowds
Solemn and noisy, rapt, tumultuous,
Sober and drunk, who carry whips and spit
Tobacco juice around and drink and eat.
The babies squall, wagons and democrats
Befog the air with dust, and oh, the heat!
Yet though these crowds will settle like the dust
In graves all over Illinois, nothing leave
Of what, or who they were, no less these crowds
Have reason at the centre like the sun;
Dimmed to the eyes this side; the sun is there!
But yet the sun knows it is there—the dust
Rises and shows the sun—there you have thought
Which is now, will be handed down of this—
These days. Oh, yes, the dust will rise at last
When evening—that's reflection, settles down;
And then you'll see a star—first magnitude,
The name is Lincoln!

                    I have read. I know.
Never in Rome or Greece were such debates,
Never in all this world. Look at the theme:
Slavery in a republic! As for men,
Where is their equal? Is it Pericles,
Demosthenes or Cicero, here with us,
Great Webster ? And the setting, think of that!
Here in this western prairie state they pass
From town to town, stand up before the mass,

And battle with their wits—set falcons loose
Of swift and ravenous logic to devour
The other's flights.   The crowds perceive the trend,
Gather enough to guide them and persuade,
But much of it is over them.   You heard
Lincoln to-day, when he had subtilized
The point to deadly ether, say to them:
"An audience like this will scarcely see
The force of what I say, but minds well trained
Will follow me and see."   That is the point.
Out of this popular oratory rises
A durable spire of truth.   This Lincoln leaves
Great thought and beauty to the race.   And yet
Douglas will be our senator, and Seward
Our President two years from now.   As Webster
Could never win the prize, this Lincoln too
Will fail to win it.

                    Why, you silly fools!
Lincoln has sprained his arms and back for good—
But he has laid the South out flat and cold,
And broken the slavocracy in two.
He did it with one question; asking that
He made the Little Giant cough and stammer,
And blush his guilt before America.
Oh, yes, he answered well enough to win
This contest here in Illinois; but look,
The Southern press is after him already,
They scent the carcass moved, withdrawn a little;

A CERTAIN POET ON THE DEBATES

They croak like buzzards—and there will be war
Between the eagles and the buzzards now,
Perhaps when Seward is elected; truly
If Lincoln should be chosen, as he won't.
It isn't that this Douglas isn't a master.
It is that he is caught between the mill-stones.
The upper is this Kansas and Nebraska,
The lower is Dred Scott—and I am glad!
Why did he father Kansas and Nebraska?
Why did he flout the ancient ordinance
Of 1787, which kept out
This curse of slavery, out of Illinois,
But brought us liberty of press and speech,
The bill of rights?   Did Congress have the power
To pass this ordinance of '87?
Or did it lack the power, because the states
That came into the union with their slaves
Might keep their slaves, reclaim as fugitive
Their slaves on freedom's soil?   Well, if it be
That Congress had the power to plaster down
The ordinance of 1787
Upon this Illinois, this great Northwest,
It had the power to say the western land
Of Kansas and Nebraska should be free
As territories ruled from Washington
And no imperialism !   So, I say again
It serves this Douglas right to be destroyed,
And ground to powder for this act of his,
This Kansas and Nebraska.

ight.
ıoop

a.
ry
!—

ites,
ruth

rue

it
s!

raska.
ur life!
h

rk
,

And can be taken to a territory,
And kept there in the face of national law
That makes the territory free.   Or else,
Were this not so, the Congress is supreme,

[75]

A CERTAIN POET ON THE DEBATES

Has slipped the chain of the organic law,
Which recognizes slavery.   What is this
But just imperialism?

      God Almighty!
They're all for freedom, a republic too.
. Kansas, Nebraska—let the people rule.
Dred Scott:—the Congress is a Parliament
Like England has, unless it pins and tucks
The constitution round its pocky body.
That may be true, but then the question is:
Is slavery charactered upon the robe,
And must the figure of the slave be seen
Wherever Congress walks?

       I'll come to that.
The point is now that Douglas has been caught
Between his Kansas and Nebraska act,
And Dred Scott never his.   And being lawful,
Obedient to the law and to the courts—
You heard him hammer Lincoln as a man
Who flouted courts—while he, the Little Giant,
Obeyed the laws—oh, yes!—So, being lawful,
As I began, must hold in level hands
Dred Scott in one, and in the other hand
This Kansas and Nebraska.

       Very good.
Lincoln has got him now, and out of all
This rhetoric, these sorties half successful,

A CERTAIN POET ON THE DEBATES

These scrimmages with Lincoln, half perplexed,
You find your Little Giant on his back
With Lincoln over him and pinning shoulders
Down to the floor.

             Here is the wrestling trick:
Can any territory keep this slavery
Out lawfully, that is, against the wish
Of any citizen? What is the answer?
If you say yes, where is Dred Scott? If no,
How do the people rule?

             What is his answer?
Why, yes, he says, a territory can
Keep slavery out. Dred Scott still sends it there,
But then the people rule, and if the people
There in Nebraska make it hot for slavery
By local law and custom, frowns and blows,
It will not thrive. That satisfied the crowd;
Enough at least, elects him Senator,
But loses him the South, the golden prize,
Splits up the country, gives us war in time,
When argument is silenced cannon boom—
And when your Seward comes to Washington
The South secedes.

             Now, listen for a moment!
What is Abe Lincoln's genealogy
In faith political? Sired by the Federalists,
And mothered by the Whigs. A tariff man;

A CERTAIN POET ON THE DEBATES

Believes too in the Bank—tariffs and banks
Filched from the plenary stores of privilege
By hands that break the shackles of the law.
He's born a Whig, has turned Republican,
What is his blood? Why, liberal construction,
Twisting the constitution out of shape,
And tearing holes in it to let the Congress
Escape and wander—where? Why, anywhere!
And though it be that touching slavery
There's nothing which forbids the Congress acting
In freedom's way—and that's the very point—
And granting that the Constitution's over
The territories, still the Congress can
Bring freedom there—this theory is akin
To loose construction, scarcely can be told
From loose construction. For you see, if freedom,
Since Congress is not hampered, can be brought,
Why not then slavery, if it be not hampered?
And why not colonies, dependencies,
Ruled just as Congress wills, if never a word
Lies in our charter to forbid or grant
The power to do it.

                    Well, there'll be a war,
And hell thereafter. So you like my talk!
What is my name? Why, Satan is my name—
And I go wandering on the earth to see,
Walk to and fro and laugh and drop a tear
In spite of all my laughter. Tears and laughter

A CERTAIN POET ON THE DEBATES

For ideas in the heads of men that seethe,
Pop, crackle, ferment, blow up bottles, kegs,
Spill and destroy bacteria on the floor
Of epochs, ruin wisdoms, cultures, faiths.
Time scrubs the floor of all such verses—Time
Matures fresh grapes, new ferments, and repeats
The old catastrophes; and hence I laugh,
And drop a tear on all the sorry waste.

PART II

THE DECISION

(*April 14th, 1861.*)

*Lincoln is sitting absorbed in thought in an office of the
executive mansion, where he has been in consultation
with his cabinet. A telegraph instrument has ceased
to click, but the wires are droning. Lincoln sud-
denly falls into a sleep, at once profound and trance-
like. In the vision members of his cabinet and secre-
taries move in and out of the room.*

LINCOLN

So there are five?

A VOICE

Yes, five to two.

SEWARD'S VOICE

A month
Has gone by and no policy. You should
Take hold yourself, or on a cabinet member
Devolve the task.

[81]

THE DECISION

LINCOLN

Whatever's to be done
Is mine to do.

SEWARD'S VOICE

Fort Sumpter leave alone!
If we employ armed force we have begun
A civil war—without armed force we fail.
We cannot take the fort and keep the fort,
Unless we subjugate the States as well.
No, let us not first draw the sword.

LINCOLN

To say—

A VOICE

Yes, five to two.

SEWARD'S VOICE

Your cabinet opposes
The Fort's provisioning.

LINCOLN

The property
And military posts, the forts which were
In our possession when the government
Came to my hands, I shall defend and hold.
I shall collect the duties, but beyond
Such things make no invasion.

A VOICE

And the mails?

[82]

THE DECISION

ANOTHER VOICE

Fort Sumpter has been shelled!

SEWARD'S VOICE

So I forewarned you.

ANOTHER VOICE

That was an error.

ANOTHER VOICE

May I ask a question?
Will you invade the country to collect
The duties, or relieve a fort alone
Where duties are in question?

LINCOLN

My inaugural—

ANOTHER VOICE

To hell with forts and duties—free the slaves!

SEWARD'S VOICE

Drop slavery! Before the people raise
The question: Is it Union or Disunion!

ANOTHER VOICE

I say to let the erring Sisters go.

ANOTHER VOICE

I care more for the principles—

[83]

THE DECISION

ANOTHER VOICE

                                Be still!
I'm sick of principles—

            THE SAME VOICE
                        The principles
Of local democratic government are worth
Twice over all the niggers.

            ANOTHER VOICE
                            Senator,
You are most eloquent when full of drink.

            ANOTHER VOICE
Would you unite the North? Maneuver them
To fire upon the Fort.

            ANOTHER VOICE
                    The time has come
To open up the question with the sword:
Is this a league, is this a nation, which?

            ANOTHER VOICE
What do you want, a tariff or a bank?
Take off your nigger mask, you centralist!

            ANOTHER VOICE
A contract broken by a signatory
Absolves the other signatory.

                [84]

THE DECISION

ANOTHER VOICE
                              Yes
The Yankee cotton spinner—

ANOTHER VOICE
                         Singing psalms!

ANOTHER VOICE
The radicals have brought us to this pass,
This agitation, hatred sectional.

DOUGLAS' VOICE
All seem to overlook this vital matter:
The President can use the military
Where only States request it.

ANOTHER VOICE
                                   You forget
The act of '75.

DOUGLAS' VOICE
                              I don't forget.
The act of '75 does not apply,
Except to laws resisted, where a marshall
Is overpowered.

ANOTHER VOICE
                    And there is no marshall,
There is no judge in the seceded States.

THE DECISION

ANOTHER VOICE

You will appoint one, so you promised.

LINCOLN

Yes.

DOUGLAS' VOICE

Then, sir, what cause is there for apprehension?
Who dares to say your President will pursue
A policy of war, unless he call
On Congress for the means and for the power?

ANOTHER VOICE

I ask about Fort Sumpter—are there ships
With cargoes of provisions on their way?—

ANOTHER VOICE

Yes, they have sailed.

OTHER VOICES

No! No!

ANOTHER VOICE

Oh, yes, the seven governors from the North
Have changed his policy. He now intends
To overthrow the federative law.
O great conspiracy—O seven-headed
Apocalyptic Beast!

*The vision grows confused. Lincoln seems to him-
self to attempt to arise from the chair but is un-*

[86]

THE DECISION

able to do so. The scene whirls about like drifting mist, struck by a sudden current of air, in which there are lights and faces. Voices are mingled together indistinguishably and then fade away. There is a silence   Out of the confusion two figures emerge, one bright, the other shadowy. Both are images of Lincoln. They become seated in a boat which is moving with great rapidity. The only sound is the droning of the telegraph.

FIRST PHANTOM

Twice have I seen this fateful scene before.

SECOND PHANTOM

The depths are moving, but no waters roar.
A mountain silence clasps the air and sea.
Look through the glassy fathoms far below:
Beneath us glides the ocean's dizzy floor
Which we skim over with a swallow's speed.

FIRST PHANTOM

I see a shadowy shore and precipices.
Yes, this portends my spirit's earthly woe.

SECOND PHANTOM

You shall not shrink ! What though your heart shall
      bleed
Its last drop out walking the abysses,
You must go forth—the hour has struck for you!

[87]

THE DECISION

The little freedoms of your life are past,
As youth may choose its work or happiness;
Now you must steer the boat through fog and blast.
This rock encircled water is no less
Than your soul captured in the trap of Fate.
Far over stands 'twixt earth and heaven a gate
Where souls depart and enter into Time,
You must set foot upon this shore and climb
And blindly your election make, renew
Your will and spirit.

FIRST PHANTOM
Tell me what to do?

SECOND PHANTOM
Heal, if you can, the nation's growing scars,
Let harmony come out of harsh discord.

FIRST PHANTOM
Suppose the seven States first draw the sword?
Have they not drawn it now?

SECOND PHANTOM
All bloody wars
Furnish great argument to place the blame
For the first blow. But even if it's blood
That blots the bond of human brotherhood,
Behold the pangs that flow from human pride
When slaughter by such blood is justified.

[88]

THE DECISION

First Phantom
What shall I do with giants who rebel?

Second Phantom
You do but traffic in a word, a name,
A word it is with which you may inflame
To mob-like fury a judicious nation—
So you may enter on an usurpation.

First Phantom
What do you say? Am I a tyrant then?

Second Phantom
Already have you thought of arming men
Without the sovereign sanction of the law.

First Phantom
But if I don't mad Treason will have gained
Such progress that it will have quite attained
Its purpose to bind down and overawe
Conciliation or resistance even.

Second Phantom
You arrogate the very will of heaven,
As tyrants do, and in your purpose find
A small reflection of the eternal mind.
What do you know of this? But if you rest
On human will and thought you must concede
A contradiction in your dream, who break
The law a rebel spirit to arrest.

[89]

THE DECISION

This is a way of sowing nettle seed.
Once you were faithful to a better creed,
That men may found new nations when the old
No longer have the people's fair consent.
Rights are not hostile. If this be a right
How may you overthrow it with your might?

FIRST PHANTOM

Have you not heard this story of me told:
At New Orleans I saw the children cry
When from the auction block their sire was sold.
I then resolved to strike this curse a blow
If ever Heaven gave
My arm the strength. It is my deepest hate.

SECOND PHANTOM

This is the thought then lying further back
In your fanatic spirit, child of woe,
Reached through a devious and hidden track!
For this you will prepare your country's grave.
You will free some, but only to enslave
A wider realm of being.

FIRST PHANTOM

                                        I would know
What may be best.

SECOND PHANTOM

                                The country is at peace.
You do not dare to ask your Congress for
Troops on the Southern people to make war.

[90]

THE DECISION

FIRST PHANTOM

I do not need to ask. I have enrolled
An oath with God the Nation to uphold.

SECOND PHANTOM

But if you call the troops will you not ask
Congress to validate your powers' increase
And sharpening of the sword for such a task?
You do not answer. Well, if this may be
Do you not contemplate a tyranny?

FIRST PHANTOM

What is this rupture but a mere defection,
What might be called rebellion, insurrection
Against the laws, which I must overthrow,
As others did before me from the first?
No word writ in the charter of the nation
Has made provision for its termination.

SECOND PHANTOM

But not to argue this—you have reversed
Your mind upon the right of revolution.

FIRST PHANTOM

Not for a righteous or a holy cause.

SECOND PHANTOM

You test it in your own soul's resolution.
But tell me when there are no writs or laws

[91]

THE DECISION

For you to execute in the Southern land
How are you acting?

First Phantom
                              But I still command
The property and forts, and other places
Belonging to the Nation.

Second Phantom
                              Understand
Their territory all such forts embraces
And sovereignty thereover is resumed.
You cannot have a war on that account,
When they would pay you for the places lost.

First Phantom
First the rebellious spirit must surmount
The barriers that keep them home with us.
They cannot leave us, cannot take and hold
What is not theirs, or what if they had sold
They could not grant.

Second Phantom
                              That is but bloody gold.
And what you say if acted on will bring
A million deaths.

First Phantom
                              They are responsible
For all the consequences if they cling
To this rebellious purpose.

[92]

THE DECISION

SECOND PHANTOM
                            To compel
This fortress's provisioning
Will be a blow first struck. It is the law:
The first blow of a war is struck by him
Who makes the first blow needful to be struck.

FIRST PHANTOM
You put the woven substance in a ruck.
I leave the issue of a war with them.
They shall not be assailed, nor may they have
Conflict with me unless they first aggress
The government.

SECOND PHANTOM
                   Oh, then they must withdraw
Resistance to your plan.

FIRST PHANTOM
                       Well, I confess
No open plan, as yet. But now attend:
I have an oath in heaven registered
The Union to preserve, protect, defend;
They have no oath the Union to destroy.

SECOND PHANTOM
What is the Union but a verbal toy
Like Justice, Beauty, Liberty or Truth?
And as for them they need not take an oath,
They need but act.

THE DECISION

First Phantom

The Union is unbroken, is a pact
Which cannot be erased or torn apart
By less than half of those who gave it breath.

Second Phantom

How does a State sink partly into death
By joining other States? Can it accede
And thereby lose its virtue to secede?

First Phantom

The Union is much older than accession.

Second Phantom

Some Union, not the Union which you rule.
The states which formed the old Confederacy
Withdrew to form the Union. Liberty
Is older than all States.
Her handmaiden has always been secession.

First Phantom

These arguments are used but to befool
The minds who loathe the wrong they would conceal.
No justice will be lost by him who waits.

Second Phantom

They ask a council for the general weal
Of all the States these matters to arrange
Without the flow of blood.

[94]

THE DECISION

FIRST PHANTOM
                                    I shall not change
What I have said: If God who rules above,
Almighty Ruler of all nations, deems
Eternal truth with them, or with our side,
That truth eternal ever must abide.

SECOND PHANTOM
But after all the truth is that which seems
The truth to you. And if mankind you love,
Why draw the sword to justify such truth?
Has any warrior of the world said more?

FIRST PHANTOM
The people may be trusted to restore
All broken rights, to them I leave all things.

SECOND PHANTOM
What do you say? These dubious wanderings
Travel along a pathway scarcely smooth.
You vowed to let no forces intermit
The Nation's laws in no place, save the means
Which should be requisite,
Were by the people from your arms withheld.
You do not let them choose when you've compelled
Their action by your act, which intervenes
Their virgin will and what you do before
You learn its voice. Yes, so arise all wars!
What people ever had a chance to voice

· THE DECISION

Free and deliberate their honest choice
'Twixt war and peace? Kings leave them to deplore
The initial step while fighting to retrieve
Or mitigate its ills. Your counselors
Have spoken, and your counselors believe
The pending step unwise. So at the last
Out of all dialectics stand two men
Each judging, each appealing to the shrine
Of God, Eternal Justice, all unknown,
Save as they see reflections of them cast
In their refracted speculations—then
What is it but the clash of sovereignties
Grown firmer from offense and wounded pride?
Yet cunning to manipulate decrees
With forethought in successive acts to hide
Provocative offenses, put in fault
The other sovereign for the first assault.

First Phantom

One man may risk his life, or suffer wrong,
He has no other but himself at stake.
A ruler has been chosen to be strong,
And save his people for his people's sake.
The clearest vision, most commanding power,
Interprets and must rule the hour,
Must call its purest sense of duty God.
Must stake its being now, in worlds to come
Before what thrones of judgment chance to be.
One phase alone of life's immensity

[96]

THE DECISION

May one o'ermaster, though it bring him doom
For things unseen, the path he never trod
Strewn with his errors. Yet he may be free
By acting through that genesis and win
Approval for the warp. No soul has room
For growth in love, but may it also thrive
To needed power in thought. If heaven require
Excess in either, while the other shrinks
In heaven's ends, should heaven then requite
The sacrifice with penitential fire?
It is enough that whosoever drinks
Of such success finds bitterness within,
The cup on earth. Can anyone begrudge
The work before me, sword that I possess?
Nor do I of another's motives judge.
If rights conflict not, yet one master right
Attuned to highest law must still prevail
And lesser laws must fail.
The winds of destiny may bear me far,
Which out of deepest heaven are arising.
I have one compass and one guiding star,
One altar for my spirit's sacrificing:
The Union is my soul's profoundest love.

Second Phantom

If you knew heaven's wish you might fulfill it,
Seen heaven's law revealed, then you might will it,
What man can say he knows the word thereof?
Oh, not alone you dedicate your life

[97]

THE DECISION

To this adventure in uncertain strife!
You give the Nation's blood and spirit too.
If you could know the Nation would renew
Its strength in years or cycles from your thought,
And through your godlike daring might be wrought
To finer triumphs in the time to come,
You would have warrant to pronounce the doom
Of blood and tears to fertilize the soil,
Where at the start revenge and hate will grow.
But what unending sorrow may recoil
Upon your purposes, who do not know?

First Phantom

What are these cliffs of purple which we near?
Gray wastes of stagnant mists above them lie.
The boat glides downward as if in a sphere
Of liquid crystal mowing, dizzily
The forked rocks point upward to the sky—
Have I then died?

Second Phantom

There is a place of moss
Whereon the prow must strike lest it be crushed.

First Phantom

This is the world's end.   How the air is hushed!

Second Phantom

Come now!   You have been ferried well across.
There!   We have landed.   Hear the whispering keel.

[98]

THE DECISION

First Phantom

I'm growing faint.

Second Phantom

Much still must I reveal.
We two must stand on yonder highest rock.

First Phantom

It cannot be!

Second Phantom

I will the door unlock.
They may not be away.   First let me knock.

(*He knocks on the cliff.   The vision grows cloudy.*)

First Phantom

What heights are these where midway to the sea
The gulls like flakes of snow eddy around!

Second Phantom

The purple wastes lie under a shorn sun.
They do not bleed, no golden ooze is seen,
No arrows pierce them.

First Phantom

And how could it be?
A barrier of mud, a sunken realm
With shores where wrecks are rotting are before you.
They sleep upon the tideless water.

[99]

THE DECISION

SECOND PHANTOM
                        Yes,
This is a quiet sea of perished dreams!

FIRST PHANTOM
Greater than Asia was this kingdom once,
But in a war it sank.

SECOND PHANTOM
                        What is the tale?

FIRST PHANTOM
There was a city set upon a hill
Which heaven governed as a pilot guides
The vessel from the stern, by force of thought.
Till spirits here were given air and light
To prove their natures, for it was the wish
Of that first pair which built its earliest hearth.
There since the husband worked with iron and fire,
Where twenty bellows blew, and all the day
The anvil sounded in a shop, which seemed .
A palace thick with stars, and giants bore
Great burdens, wielded sledges, and obeyed
The master workman, so the city heaped
Great store of armament and priceless works.
Meanwhile the woman in whose eyes and brow
The final reason, compress of all light
Made of all lights absorbed, resolved, and tamed
Lay like a high serenity of power,
Or balanced wisdom, bore great sons to rule

[100]

THE DECISION

The state and to preserve it in the wars
When wars should come. In peace to keep the courts,
And laws like to their mother's face, a face
Which awed the dullest slave, out of whose brain
The idea like a statue carved in rock
By hammers broken, rolled, beholding it.
She taught her sons that some are born to rule,
And some to serve, and some to carry torches,
And some to blow the bellows for the fire
Where torches may be lit; and how a state
Where high and low remain as high and low
So long as nature wills, move in a sphere
Of democratic laws, where all may have
The bread they earn, and where no strength may seize
Another's happiness, another's bread.
Hence was it that she fired her sons to drive
A giant troubler from the city's gates,
And shut him up in Sicily.

                              But the land
Over whose hills and vales the waters lie
There where we look had other life. I speak:
It was a land of many lakes and rivers,
And plains and meadows, mountains full of ore,
Both gold and silver, copper, precious stones.
And valued wood, most fruitful of all things,
Herbage or roots, or corn, whatever gives
Delight or sustenance. And the ruler's strength
Brought riches from all ports. But to relate

THE DECISION

Its founder's part, the country was divided
Among ten rulers who had sworn to obey
Injunctions carven on a shaft of gold,
Erected in the middle of the realm.
And here the people of the several States
Gathered for conference on the general weal,
And to inquire if any of the states
Had trespassed on the other, or transgressed
The writing on the shaft of gold, and pass
Appropriate judgment; for upon the shaft
Curses were graven on the recreant.
And it was written none should take up arms
Against the other; and if one should raise
His hand against the central strength (for where
The shaft of gold stood, there a palace stood
Where lived a ruler speaking for them all),
Then should the others rescue it and fling
The rebels back.

                   Such was this empire lost
And so did it remain so long as men
Obeyed the laws and heaven loved. At first
They practiced wisdom, they despised all things
Save virtue only, lightly thought of gold,
Were sober, hated luxury, knew control
Of passions and of self. And knew that wealth
Grows with such virtues, and by unity
With one another, but by zeal for wealth
All friendship dies. And so they waxed in store

THE DECISION

Of gold and spirit. But at last the soul,
Which was divine and moved in them, fell off
And weakened, grew diluted with too much
Of human nature, and became unjust,
Cruel and base, voracious, drunken, lost
To wisdom, discipline; and the seeing eye
Saw all good things forgotten, but to those
Who had no eye to see true happiness
They still appeared most blest and glorious,
Filled as they were with avarice and lust.
So then arose one state, and then another
Against the central ruler, none was free
Of disobedience to the graven words
Upon the shaft of gold, until at last
The city on the hill watching the strife
Embarked with troops.

SECOND PHANTOM
                    Have you not prophesied
Your country's fate if you assault the South?
It is the zeal for wealth that cries for war.
From such a war our spirit shall be lost,
Our justice fouled, our friendship turned to hate,
Our laughter rendered drunken. We shall be
The city on the hill, the island lost—
Have both not perished?

FIRST PHANTOM
                    Stay! It is enough
To live amid the misery of today,

[103]

THE DECISION

Without this contemplation of the past.
What is this sky, this earth to which we come?
This nothingness, this substance, air and rock
Which to our life is hard reality
And to our thought a dream?   All nature sings,
Creates, rejoices, man alone has life
In pain as life, unfolding life as pain,
As if a child could live but never be
Delivered from the womb.   And for myself
What am I but a creature, heart and head,
Hands reaching up to catch at rock or bough?
Hands, heart and head of flesh, immortal fire,
With feet unshapen, still a part of earth
Where from that undistinguished mass of clay
Hands, heart and head would pluck them?   I could faint,
Fly from the task before me but for this:
The will which when confronted bares its face
And says go on, or lie down with the beasts
In silence and corruption.   Let me look
No more upon this sea!

SECOND PHANTOM
                    Where shall we go?

FIRST PHANTOM
To some place less disquieting, more secure.

(They leave the heights and descend,
approaching a mysterious place
where heaven and earth are connected by gates.)

[104]

THE DECISION

First Phantom
I can no further walk or fly.

Second Phantom
You enter at these gates near by.

First Phantom
I fall through space. Your hand, my friend.

Second Phantom
Quietly like a star descend.

(*They pass through the gates into a meadow.*)

First Phantom
What is this meadow which I see?

Second Phantom
Here come the souls of men to be.
Can you remember what you said
Among the living and the dead:
I would know heaven's deepest law
And flood the world of men with light,
I would bring justice and be just.

First Phantom
Out of each soul's prenatal night
Something of what you say returns.
The soul descending into dust
Loses its memory as it burns
Less brightly when the spirit wanes.

[105]

THE DECISION

SECOND PHANTOM

Behold that pillar of splendor shining
And bound to earth and heaven by chains!
You see the distaff to it fixed
And in the distaff whorls of iron,
Each rising to a higher rim,
And on each whirling rim a siren
Chants, as you hear, her solemn hymn.

FIRST PHANTOM

I hear it with the singing mixed
Of one upon whose giant knee
The distaff turns to hands that reach
From thrones which stand at equal spaces.

SECOND PHANTOM

The giant is Necessity,
The Fates are reaching from the thrones

FIRST PHANTOM

Such garlands for such darkened faces!
What are these solemn monotones,
Which are not music, are not speech?

SECOND PHANTOM

They labor through Eternity.
The Universe of visible things
Turns with the distaff here again.
The dead come back with questionings

[106]

THE DECISION

Of earthly failure, loss or pain,
And would choose better than before.
Some say that Agamemnon chose
The loneliness of eagle wings
In hatred of his mortal woes.

FIRST PHANTOM

From dreams like these I must be free! I know,
Dread phantom, you are nothing but myself.
You stand before me lately, mocking elf,
Too much, and follow me where'er I go.
What this portends I know not, death I fear.
But what seems just to do I shall perform.
A nation's destiny is mine to steer,
A people's hope is on me in the storm.
Behind these voices when they sing or laugh
I hear the droning of the telegraph:
Come! I would study now the last dispatches.

SECOND PHANTOM

No meaning it is clear your soul attaches
To thrones, or sirens, or the giant knees.
You have not fixed upon a policy.

FIRST PHANTOM

I shall be guided—

SECOND PHANTOM

By necessity—

[107]

THE DECISION

First Phantom
Well, yes, but by the will of God as well.

Second Phantom
How can you tell it from the will of hell?

(*Voices from the thrones.*)

First Throne
Here I sit spinning
From what beginning
Did I begin?

Second Throne
Give me the thread!
I will assign him
Grief to refine him,
Thorns for his head.
Toil never ending
Up from his birth
This shall be leaven
To lift him from earth
Up into heaven.

(*Many souls are crowded into
the meadow. A figure takes
from the lap of Lachesis lots
and scatters them.*)

Second Phantom
Who honors heaven, heaven wins.

[108]

THE DECISION

Not here your fate on earth begins.
I only show you where you stood
Amid the fates and now your work
Of justice and of brotherhood.
You're weary, yet you cannot shrink
The task assumed—how it increases!
A giant hand thrust in releases
The numbered lots of mortal life,
There from the apron of Lachesis,
And throws them to the multitude
Awaiting mortal strife.

SECOND THRONE

One fluttered to his hand.   He ran
Between the thrones, the distaff under
Which swayed and rolled upon her knees.
The chains that bound it clanked and creaked.
The far-off depths the lightening streaked
Uprolled the deep symphonic thunder
Which rumbled like a chariot, till
Its echoes died and all was still,
Save for the tinkling pipe and purl
As faster sped the seventh whorl.
We nodded, laughing at the game,
And said: He's dreaming Pericles
Who gave his soul to ancient Greece.
What will he do with such a name?

SECOND PHANTOM

Do you remember?

THE DECISION

FIRST PHANTOM

                                    I remember
A dream I had in early youth:
My birth was humble, still I dreamed
To consecrate my life to Truth
And for the truth to be esteemed.
I love the Republic, I would see
Its soil and all its people free!

(*The Furies enter.*)

THE THRONES

Heaven and God are under us.   Reveal
We never may what end the law achieves.
He shall be free who with increasing zeal
Still labors and believes.

THE FURIES

You may deceive this fellow with such stuff;
We have seen history woven long enough
To know the good men plan at least by half
Results in evil.

THE THRONES

                          Be the epitaph
Of him who moulds his being by this thought:
"He doubted, failure marked the work he wrought."

THE FURIES

What is the law, then, that he must obey?

THE DECISION

The Thrones

The law that has most universal sway.

The Furies

What may that be? Is it to choose the good?

The Thrones

You know his dream of human brotherhood.

The Furies

He must seize power such dreams to realize.
In usurpation great corruption lies.

First Phantom

What is this shape I deal with? It is whole,
Inseparable forever, with a soul.
It is a life of undivided breath.
To break its body is to give it death.

The Furies

There might be two souls where before was one.

First Phantom

From heaven's battlements a clarion
Shivers the mystic chords of memory,
Stretched forth from every grave and battle-field,
My life may pay the forfeit—let it be.
Destroy me if you will, I shall not yield
To anarch forces.

THE DECISION

Then by tyranny
You'll break the giants if they dare rebel.
Men through the giants only may be free.
Destroy them or enchain them and you quell
The Titan powers by whom there came
Freedom's Promethean flame.

The Thrones

Whence is the Voice,
Which sings the eternal theme
Of giants whirled
Beneath the thunderbolts of Strength supreme;
Of angels who have made the fateful choice,
From heaven headlong hurled?
Of Odin, in Valhalla, keeping guard
Against the malice of the giant world,
Slaying the mighty Ymir?
And what was their reward
Who warred upon the Thunderer
For sovereignty for pity of mankind?—
Go bear in pain the burden of the earth,
Or under mountains blind
Breathe hateful fire,
Or moan your agony and fallen wrath
Chained to the rocks,
So shall thought rule, not force, or their desire
Which is the law of music not of bread
Or lower ordinance. Do you now tread,

[112]

THE DECISION

Mortal, the path of service to the race?
Do you bring fire, or quell disharmony,
Destroy the Titans?   In all time and space
Freedom is only for the wise and free!

The Thrones

A hand like lightning from a thunder cloud
Reaches from heaven to the apron's folds,
And takes the inscrutable lots,
And scatters them among the spectral crowd.
On them are written labors, wars and plots.
Thus are they thrown, like snow they fall where'er
They may be driven by the unseen air,
Which moves so thinly here no eye beholds
Its coming and its going.   They shall fall
Where chance may govern.   Look!   These two shall find
Their fate and incarnation, work above
This meadow under earth.   Not wholly blind
Shall they select the soul they would be like—
That they may will in part—the rest shall be
Ruled by the working of a destiny
Of our appointing when the hour shall strike
Commissioned under seal to say "Arise
The hour has struck."

First Phantom
My other self, your hand.

Second Phantom
We must be one, not two.

THE DECISION

First Phantom

We must not stand
In strength, intentions, visions separate.

(The two phantoms become one.)

The Thrones

O soul, now one which just before was two,
What is your deepest love?

The Phantom

It is the True.

I love the Right, the Good, confederate
And in this order, ruling, not apart:
If this may be, mind, conscience, heart
In harmony and balanced equipoise,
I would possess, and I would have a voice
To sway with truth.

The Thrones

Choose then O soul your fate!

The Phantom

Down bending I obey. What have I done?

First Throne

Come Destiny and overwatch your son.

The Destiny

Behold I loved and kept the public good
Forever in my eye   At my command
Were many armies, cities, islands, realms
Which I ruled over with a master hand.

[114]

THE DECISION

And where I could not lead by gentle word
I forced compliance, so my power withstood
Internal quarrels and the foreign sword.
But when I left the life of earth they came
Around my bed, a worthy group, and spoke
My trophies and authority and fame.
Not one took notice of my greatest deeds:
No father's heart for my fault ever broke,
Nor wailing woman tore her widow's weeds.
Law, Freedom, Progress, Virtue, Beauty, Truth,
Humility, Religion, Knowledge lay
Along the pathway of my city's youth.
Ill fortune forced imperial temptation
And these divided even by heaven sundered
Leaving to Empire and to Riches sway
O'er Beauty, Knowledge, Progress, till the day
Of hatred, envy, bitter disputation,
All good was sunk. Its walls and temples thundered,
My city on the hill was crushed and fell
Through lust of riches, from its elevation.
Study my problem and my spirit well.
Yours are not greatly different—beware
Great riches for your country lest they come
With weakness and debasement for a snare.
And to this end curb studied greed and those
Spirits luxurious, and adventuresome,
And those unjust, their hatred, guile oppose.
Right is a thing 'twixt equals, and the strong
Do what they can, the weak must suffer wrong.

[115]

THE DECISION

Therefore the balance hold for all, assuage
The fury and revenge which yet may rage
Around your fallen brothers, when you ride
Triumphant.

SECOND THRONE
　　　　　Now conduct him to our side
Beneath the distaff in my hand.
Thus is his fate forever ratified.

(*The Image Passes.*)

THIRD THRONE
Now hither bring him,—thus I breathe my spell.
His doom is now made irreversible.

THE THRONE OF NECESSITY
Pass under me.　Now of this cup drink deep.
There, he has drunk it and so falls in sleep.
Now guard him, Destiny!

(*A sound of cannon.　Lincoln awakes.　The Secretary of War enters.*)

THE SECRETARY OF WAR
Fort Sumter has been fired on!

LINCOLN
　　　　　Call the troops!

PART III

LINCOLN MAKES A MEMORANDUM

(*November 23rd, 1864.*)

"The will of God prevails. In great contests each party claims to act in accordance with the will of God. Both may be, and one must be wrong. God cannot be for and against the same thing at the same time. In the present Civil War it is quite possible that God's purpose is something different from the purpose of either party; and yet the human instrumentalities, working just as they do, are of the best adoption to effect his purpose. I am almost ready to say that this is probably true; that God wills this contest, and wills that it shall not end yet. By his mere great power on the minds of the now contestants he could have either saved or destroyed the Union without a human contest. Yet the contest began. And having begun he could give the final victory to either side any day. Yet the contest proceeds."

WINTER GARDEN THEATRE

(*New York, November 23rd, 1864.*) JOHN WILKES
BOOTH *is speaking behind the scenes to his brother.*)

If you—if you had told me this before,
If I had known of it—if I had known,
I had not played to-night, no, by the gods,
I had not played Marc Antony, nor heard
You speak the words of Brutus. You—my brother,
You nursed in liberty—you nourished upon
Great thoughts and dreams, have soiled me, soiled the
    name
Of Booth, our father's name. Yes, you have soiled
All spirits free, all lofty souls, the soul
Of Brutus and of Shakespeare. Why, till now
Conceal from me your vote for Lincoln—why?
Why? In your heart of hearts you are ashamed,
And loose the secret now for penitence!
For you have helped the hand that wrecks and slays
Who will be king and on these ruined States
Erect a throne. He who commenced this war,
And broke the law to do it. He who struck
The liberty of speech and of the press;
He who tore up the ancient writ of freemen,

And filled the jails against the law. Lincoln!
Into whose ears the shrieks of horror rise
From Gettysburg, Manassas—yet who says
The will of God be done, for him you vote!
And walk these boards to-night and live the soul
Of Brutus, speak his words—Oh! "Had you rather
Cæsar were living and die all slaves than
That Cæsar were dead to live all freemen." God!
You had this secret in your breast the while:
This vote for Lincoln, and these words of Brutus
Blown from the Shakespeare trumpet to our ears,
Hearts, consciences, meant what to you—meant what?
Words for an actor, words for a lisping girl
Repeating them by rote! But why not truth
For men to live by, to be taken into
The beings of men for living? Oh, my God—
I hate you and I leave you. I shall never
Look on your face again!

THE SPARROW HAWK IN THE RAIN

(ALEXANDER STEPHENS *hears news.*)

(*Liberty Hall, April 9th, 1865.*)

That's done! And well, I'd rather not have gone
To take such news. But now I'm glad you picked me—
I saw and heard him. I was ushered in,
And after hems and haws, I said at last,
"Lee has surrendered."

                              What a face he had
When I said that: "Lee has surrendered." Once,
When I was just a boy, I shot a sparhawk,
Just tore his breast away, and did not kill him.
He hopped up to a twig and perched, I peered
Through bushes for my victim—there he was
His breast shot all away, so I could see
His heart a-beating—but the sparhawk's eyes
Were bright as dew, with pain! I thought of this
When I saw Alec Stephens, said to him,
"Lee has surrendered."

                              There the midget sat
His face as wrinkled as thin cream, as yellow

THE SPARROW HAWK IN THE RAIN

As squirrel skin—But ah, that piercing eye!
As restless as my sparhawk's, not with moving
But just with light, such pained uneasiness.
So there he sat, a thin, pale, little man,
Wrapped in a monstrous cloak, as wide and dark
As his own melancholy—I shed tears
For such soul sickness, sorrow and such eyes,
That breast all shot away, that heart exposed
For eyes to see it beat, those burning eyes!

I stood there with my hat within my hand,
Said: "Mr. Stephens, I have come to tell you,
Lee has surrendered." He just looked at me
Then in a thin, cracked voice he said at once,
"It had to come." That's all, "It had to come."
"Pray have a seat," he added. For you see
He's known me for some years, I am his friend.
"It had to come." He only said that once.
Then, after silence, he chirped up again:
"I knew when I came back from Hampton Roads
It soon would be. Home-coming is the thing
When all is over in the world you've loved,
And worked with. And this Liberty Hall is good.
My sleeplessness is not so tiring here,
My pain more tolerable, and as for thought,
That goes on anywhere, and thought is life,
And while I think, I live."

      He paused a minute,
I took a seat, enthralled with what he said,

[121]

THE SPARROW HAWK IN THE RAIN

A sparhawk in the rain, breast torn away,
His beating heart in view, his burning eyes!
"But everyone will see, the North will see,
Our cause was theirs, the South's cause was the cause
Of everyone both north and south. They'll see
Their liberties not long survive our own.
There is no difference, and cannot be
Between empire, consolidation, none
Between imperialism, centralism, none!"

I saw he was disposed to talk, let fall
My hat upon the floor. There in that cloak
All huddled like a child he sat and talked
In that thin voice. Bent over, hands on knees,
I listened like a man bewitched.

                                            He said:
"As I am sick, cannot endure the strain
Of practice at the bar, am face to face
With silence after thunder, after war,
This terrifying calm, and after days
Top full of problems, duties in my place
In the South, vice-president, adviser,
Upon insoluble things, now after these
I cannot sit here idle, so I plan
To write a book. For, if I tell the truth,
My book will live, will be a shaft of granite
Which guns can never batter. First, perhaps,
I'll have to go to prison, let it be.
The North is now a maniac—here I am,

THE SPARROW HAWK IN THE RAIN

Easy to capture, but I'll think in prison,
Perhaps they'll let me write, but anyway
I'll try to write a book and answer questions.

"A soldier at Manassas shot to death
Asked, as he died, 'What is it all about?'
Thousands of boys, I fancy, asked the same
Dying at Petersburg and Antietam,
Cold Harbor, Gettysburg. I'll answer them.
I'll dedicate the book to all true friends
Of Liberty wherever they may be,
Especially to those with eyes to look
Upon a federation of free states as means
Surest and purest to preserve mankind
Against the monarch principle."

                              Just then
A darkey came to bring him broth, he drank
And I arose to go. He waved his hand
And asked me: "Would you like to hear about
The book I plan to write?"

                          I longed to stay
And hear him talk, but feared to tire him out.
I hinted this, he smiled a little smile
And said: "If I'm alone, I think, and thought
Without you talk it out is like a hopper
That is not emptied and may overflow,
Or choke the grinding stones. Be seated, sir,
If you would please to listen."

THE SPARROW HAWK IN THE RAIN

                                        So I stayed.
When he had drunk the broth, he settled back
To talk to me and tell me of his book,
A sparhawk, as I said, with burning eyes!
"First I will show the nature of the league,
The compact, constitution, the republic
Called federative even by Washington.
I only sketch the plan to you. Take this:
States make the Declaration, therefore states
Existed at the time to make it. States
Signed up the Articles of Confederation
In seventeen seventy-eight, and to what end?
Why for 'perpetual union.' Was it so?
No, nine years after, states, the very same
Withdrew, seceded from 'perpetual union'
Under the Articles and acceded to,
Ratified, what you will, the Constitution,
And formed not a 'perpetual union' but
'More perfect union.'

                              "If there is a man
Or ever was more gifted with the power
Of cunning words that reach the heart than Lincoln,
I do not know him. Don't you see it wins,
Captures the swelling feelings to declare
The Union older than the states?—it's false,
But Lincoln says it. Here's another strain
That moves the mob: 'The Constitution has
No word providing for its own destruction,

THE SPARROW HAWK IN THE RAIN

The ending of the government thereunder.'
This Lincoln is a sophist, and in truth
With all this moral cry against the curse
Of slavery and these arguments of Lincoln
We were put down, just as a hue and cry
Will stifle Reason; but you can be sure
Reason will have her way and punishment
Will fall for her betrayal.

                      "Let us see:
'Was there provisions in the Articles
Of that perpetual union for the end
Of that perpetual union? Not at all!
How did these states then end it? By seceding
To form a better one! Is there provision
For getting out, withdrawing from the Union
Formed by the Constitution? No! Why not?
Could not states do what they had done before,
Leave 'a more perfect union,' as they left
'Perpetual union?' What's a state in fact?
A state's a sovereign, look in Vattell, look
In any great authority. So a sovereign
May take back what it delegated, mark you,
Not what it deeded, parted with, but only
Delegated. In regard to that
All powers not delegated were reserved.
Well, to resume, no word is in the charter
To end the charter. And a contract has
No word to end it by, how do you end it?
You end it by rescinding, when one party

Has broken it. Is this a contract, compact?
Even the mighty Webster said it was.
And further, if the Northern States, he said,
Refuse to carry in effect the part
Respecting restoration of fugitive slaves,
The South would be no longer bound to keep—
What did he say? the *compact,* that's the word!
Next then, what caused the war? I'll show and prove
It was not slavery of the blacks, but slavery
The North would force on us. For seventy years
Fierce, bitter conflict waged between the forces
Of those who would maintain the Federal form,
And those who would absorb in the Federal head
All power of government; between the forces
Of sovereignty in the people and control,
And sovereignty in a central hand. Why, look,
No sooner was the perfect union formed
Than monarchists began to play their arts
Through tariffs, banks, assumption bills, the Act
That made the Federal Courts. And none of these
Had warrant in the charter; yet you see
They overleaped its bounds. And so it was
To make all clear, explicit, when we framed
For these Confederate States our charter, we
Forbade expressly tariffs, meant to foster
Industrial adventures.

                              "No, my friend,
Our slavery was not the cause of war.

THE SPARROW HAWK IN THE RAIN

They would have Empire and the slavery
That comes from it: unlicensed power to deal
With fortunes, lives, economies and rights.
We fought them in the Congress seventy years;
We fought them at the hustings, with the ballot;
And when they shouldered guns, we shouldered guns,
And fought them to the last—now we have lost,
And so I write my book.

                                "What is the difference
Between a mob, an army shouting God,
Fired by a moral erethism fixed
On slaughter for the triumph of its dream,
A riddance of its hate—what is the difference
Between an army like this and a man
Who dreams God moves, inspires him to an act
Of foul assassination? None at all!
Why, there's your Northern army shouting God,
Your pure New England with its tariff spoils,
Its banks and growing wealth, uplifting hands,
Invoking God against us till they flame
A crazy party and a maddened army,
To war upon us. But if slavery
Be sinful, where's the word of Christ to say
That slavery is sinful? Not a word
From him who scourged the Scribes and Pharisees
For robbing widows' houses, but no word
Against the sin of slavery. Yet behold
He found no faith in all of Israel

THE SPARROW HAWK IN THE RAIN

To equal that—of whom?—a man who owned
Slaves, as we did. I mean the Centurion.
And is this all? St. Paul who speaks for God
With equal inspiration with New England,
As I should judge, enjoins the slaves to count
Their masters worthy of all honor, that
God and his doctrine be not blasphemed.

                                        "But
If it be wrong to hold as property
A service, even a man to keep the service—
Let us be clear and fair—then is it wrong
To hold indentures of apprenticeship?
And if, as Lincoln says, it is a right
Given of God for every man to have,
Eat if he will the bread he earns, then God
Is blasphemed in the North where labor's paid
Not what it earns, but what it must accept,
Chained by necessity, and so enslaved.
And all these tariff laws are slavery
By which my bread is taken, all the banks
That profit by their issues, special rights,
Enslave us, in the future will enslave
Both North and South, when darkeys shall be free
To choose their masters, but must choose, no less.
Take what the master hand consents to pay,
And eat what bread is given. Yes, you know
Our slavery was a gentle thing, belied
As bloody, sullen, selfish—yet you know

THE SPARROW HAWK IN THE RAIN

It was a gentle thing, a way to keep
A race inferior in a place of work,
Duly controlled. For once that race is freed
It will go forth to mingle, mix and wed
With whites and claim equality, the ballot,
Places of trust and profit, judgment seats.
Lincoln denies he favors this, no less
We'll come to that. And all the while the mills
And factories in the North will bring to us
The helpless poor of Europe, and enslave them
By pauper wages, and enslave us all
With tariff-favored products. Slavery!
God's curse is on us for our Slavery!
What do you think?

                    "They say we broke the law,
Were rebels, insurrectionists; I'll treat
Those subjects in my book. But let us see,
They did not keep the law; they had their banks,
They had their tariffs, they infracted laws
Respecting slaves who ran away, they joined
Posses and leagues to break those laws, and we
In virtue of these breaches, were released
From this, the compact, just as Webster says.
Did Lincoln keep the law and keep his oath
The Constitution to support, obey?
He did not keep it, and he broke his oath.
Did he have lawful power to call the troops?
Did he have lawful warrant to blockade

THE SPARROW HAWK IN THE RAIN

Our southern ports? No one pretends he did.
His Congress by a special act made valid
These tyrant usurpations. Had he power
To strike the habeas corpus, gag the press?—
No power at all—he only seized the power
To reach what he conceived was all supreme,
The saving of the Union—more of this.
Well, then, what are these words: You break the law
On those who break it and confess they do?
You have two ideas: Union and Secession,
Or two republics made from one, that's all.
And those who think secession criminal
Turn criminals themselves to stay the crime,
And shout the Union. To this end I come,
This figment called the Union, which obsessed
The brain of Lincoln.

              "For the point is this,
You may take Truth or Liberty or Union
For a battle cry, kill and be killed therefor,
But if our reasons rule, if we are men,
We take them at our peril. We must stake
Our souls upon the choice, be clear of mind
That what we cry as Truth is Truth indeed,
That Liberty is Liberty, that the Union
Is not a noun, a word, a subtlety,
But is a status, substance, living temple
Reared from the bottom up on stones of fate,
Predestined. Yet the truth is only this:

[130]

THE SPARROW HAWK IN THE RAIN

The Union is a noun and nothing more,
And stands for what? A federative thing
Formed of the wills of states, not otherwise.
Existing; and to kill to save the Union
Is but the exercise of a hue and cry,
An arbitrary passion, sophist's dream.
And Robespierre, who killed for liberty,
And Cæsar, who destroyed the Roman liberties
To have his way, are of the quality
Of Lincoln, whom I know. Take Robespierre,
Was he not by a sense of justice moved,
Pure, and as frigid as a bust of stone?
And Cæsar had devoted friends, and Cæsar,
The accomplished orator, general and scholar,
Charming and gentle in his private walks,
Destroyed the hopes of Rome.

                              "Now, mark me friend,
I do not think that Lincoln meant to crush
The institutions of his country—no,
His fault was this—the Union, yes the noun,
Rose to religious mysticism, and enthralled
With sentiment his soul. And his ideas
Of its formation, structure in his logic
Rested upon a subtle solecism.
And for this noun, in spite of virtues great
Of head and heart, he used his other self,
His Cæsar self, his self of Robespierre,
In the great office which he exercised,

THE SPARROW HAWK IN THE RAIN

To bring us Oak Hill, Corinth, Fredericksburg.
Think you, if when he kept the store at Salem
A humble, studious man, he had been told
He would make wails of horror, wake the cries
Of pestilence and famine in the camps,
Bring devastation, rapine, fire and death—
Had he been told this, he had said—'My soul!
Never,' and with Hazael said, 'Behold,
Is thy servant a dog, that he should do this thing?'
Power changes men! And when the people give
Power or surrender it, they scarcely know
The thing they give, surrender.

                        "But I ask
What is there in the Union, what indeed
In any government's supremacy
Or maintenance that justifies these acts—
These horrors, slaughters—near a million men
Slaughtered for what? The Union. Treasure spent
Beyond all counting for the Union. When
No life had been destroyed, no dollar spent
If they had let us go, left us alone
To go our way. You see they did to us
What England did; succeeded, where she failed.
And thus you see that human life is cheap,
And suffering a sequence when a dream,
An Idea takes a man, a mob, an army.
Which makes our life a jest, our boasted Reason
An instrument too weak for savagery.
Then for the rest—you see—I think you see.—"

[132]

THE SPARROW HAWK IN THE RAIN

Sleep now was taking him. My little sparhawk
Was worn out, and his eyes began to droop,
His voice to fail him. In a moment then
He sank down in his cloak and fell asleep—
And I arose and left.

ADELAIDE AND JOHN WILKES BOOTH

(At the National Hall, Washington, April 9th, 1865.)

ADELAIDE

Yes, even this you can surmount by art,
Lee has surrendered, but—

BOOTH

              No! all is lost.
God judge me, right or wrong, but never man.
I love peace more than life, have loved the Union.
Have waited for the clouds to break, have prayed
For justice, peace; but now all hope is dead.
My prayers are futile, as my hopes have been.
God's will be done. I go to see and share
The end, though bitter.

ADELAIDE

            John! you must be calm.

BOOTH

I am most calm, but fixed.

ADELAIDE

            You are not calm;
Strange light is in your eyes, your face is pale.
You cannot stretch your hands out but they tremble.

[134]

ADELAIDE AND JOHN WILKES BOOTH

You have avoided me, you walk alone,
Sup, sit alone, lest concentrated thought,
This thought of yours be turned aside. My friend,
Take Beauty in your heart to heal its hurts.
Art is for you. You are a son of Art—
Why waste your spirit on such things as these?
Rulers and nations pass, and wars are lost,
Their issues are forgotten, pushed aside—
Art is eternal and the sons of Art
Live in its calm, above the dust and sweat
Of politics and statecraft. O my friend,
Why should this Brutus, the tyrranicide,
The patriot, move you so; and why not Brutus
As a soul made clear by Shakespeare for your Art
To glory in and re-create for men
To see what Brutus was?

BOOTH
                        Why, what is this
But playing with life, that's all it is to play,
Hard play at that, to sleep, to walk, to rest
For strength to trip the stage and imitate
The soul of Brutus! If it be so much,
Art as you say, to live him on the stage,
What would it be to live him to the life,
And do his act in deed?

ADELAIDE
                        What do you say?
John, you are mad! So that is in your heart!
[135]

ADELAIDE AND JOHN WILKES BOOTH

Look! pause! and muster all your strength of mind,
Forecast, survey—fly from yourself—away—
Even for a week withdraw your mind from this—
That you may see, return with freshened mind
To look upon the horror that you plot.
John, by the love you woke in me for beauty
Of face and genius, listen, on my knees
I ask you, pause and think!

BOOTH
                            But I have thought.
I know I shall be hated by the North,
And doubted in the South, it may be, yet
God's will be done. For in a day to come
My name will shine as shines the name of Brutus,
Whose spirit is in me and speaks to me.
Could you have seen, as I have seen, the woes
And horrors of this war in every state,
Then you would pray, as I have prayed, to God
To give the Northern mind pity and justice,
And dry this sea of blood. Alas! my country!
What is this trifling Art beside my country,
This rhetoric spoken, memorized? My friend,
I would have given a thousand lives to see
My country whole, unbroken. Even now
I'd give my life to see her what she was,
Before this man, this tyrant, bloody Cæsar,
This Cæsar worse than Cæsar, who—behold,

ADELAIDE AND JOHN WILKES BOOTH

In the name of God—why, think in the name of God
Made her a pitiless sovereignty, a force
As cold as steel, and dragged her glorious flag
Through cruelty, oppression, till its stripes
Are bloody gashes on the face of heaven.
How I have loved that flag! How I have longed
To see it flap free from the scarlet mist
That spoils its glory. As for me, this country
Which I loved as a lover loves his bride,
Seems now a dream! The South has all my love,
What has it done? Withdrawn, and that alone,
From the Union which was formed by states withdrawing
From the old confederacy, and leaving states
Out in the cold that did not wish to join.
What has the South done that it might not do
Under the Declaration? Then to think
That all these tens of thousands of our kin,
Our blood, our brothers, should be massacred
For loving God and Liberty, serving God.
And now this day! The South is crushed at last,
The negroes freed by what?—by force, by force
Which John Brown used, and for the which he paid
With his damned neck! O Reason! Adelaide,
Of all men I am sanest, they are mad
Who cannot see these truths: that slavery
Is sanctioned by the Creator, read St. Paul;
That men may revolutionize, as matter of right,
Secede from what they have acceded to,

And not be murdered for it. Do you think
I have not measured motives, thoughts? My friend,
I could be happy, if I could forget
The duty laid upon me, have the means
For happiness, so many friends and you,
Great competence and fame, and greater fame
In store for deeper art. So much for this!
As for the South, as citizens, persons, love
The South is not my friend. Then there's my mother,
Whom I adore: See what I sacrifice:
Fame, money, friends, my mother—and for what?
Were it the South, I should not think to act—
But it is God, is Justice, and I love
God, Justice, more than wealth or fame, yes more
Than home or mother. All is lost at last.
The South has been erased and is no more.
The Republic of the North and South is dead,
Gutted by a guerilla. Yes, my country
Has vanished from the earth and is no more,
I have no wish to live, my country being
Dead and a stench.

ADELAIDE

    I put my arms around you—
Be patient—listen—do not thrust me off—
John—

BOOTH
You must not hold me, Adelaide—farewell.
[138]

ADELAIDE AND JOHN WILKES BOOTH

ADELAIDE

John! John!

BOOTH

God calls me—I obey!

(*He goes out.*)

BRUTUS LIVES AGAIN IN BOOTH

(*Ford's Theatre, Good Friday, April 14th, 1865.*)

FIRST STAGE HAND

What time is it?

SECOND STAGE HAND

Time for the curtain nearly.

FIRST STAGE HAND

There's Miss Keene in the wings

(*The orchestra starts up; the audience sings*:

Honor to our soldiers,
Our Nation's greatest pride,
Who 'neath our Starry Banner's folds,
Have fought, have bled and died.
They're Nature's noblest handiwork,
No king as proud as they.
God bless the heroes of the land,
And cheer them on their way.

[140]

BRUTUS LIVES AGAIN IN BOOTH

Scene II.   The White House.

Colfax   *Oglesby*   *Lincoln*

LINCOLN

This for you, Colfax.

> (*Hands him a pass*)

                   Come in at nine to-morrow.
I'm off soon for the theatre with my wife—
A little party.   Grant was going too;
Has changed his mind, goes north with Mrs. Grant.
There'll be an audience to see the hero
Of Appomatox.

OGLESBY

               Well, rather you, I think
Who picked Grant for the work, and brought the war
To end, as it has ended.

LINCOLN

                      Oh, not me.
I am familiar as an old shoe here.
I'd say the war is ending.   There may be
Some battle yet.

COLFAX

Mere sputterings of the flame.

LINCOLN

Well, something's on.   I had my dream last night
Which I have had before, so often, always

[141]

BRUTUS LIVES AGAIN IN BOOTH

Before some great event: I'm in a boat,
And swiftly move toward a shadowy shore.
I had this dream preceding Bull Run, Vicksburg,
Gettysburg, Antietam. It may be
A battle's on this minute. I think so.
It must relate to Sherman. For I know
No other great event to follow my dream.

OGLESBY

Our dreams are made of days lived long ago:
Your boat's perhaps your flat boat at New Salem.

COLFAX

I'm happy to live now, the war is won.
God bless you, Mr. President, keep you too.

LINCOLN

You will excuse me, gentlemen. I go,
For Mrs. Lincoln waits.

(*He goes out.*)

OGLESBY

                                The other day
Lincoln was with Charles Sumner down the James,
Was reading Shakespeare, read aloud three times
Those lines which read: "Duncan is in his grave,
After life's fitful fever he sleeps well;
Treason has done his worst: nor steel nor poison,
Malice domestic, foreign levy, nothing
Can touch him further."

[142]

BRUTUS LIVES AGAIN IN BOOTH

COLFAX

          Did you note to-night
He looked those words: "Nothing can touch him
    further"?
These months before how ghastly gray his face!
What droop of melancholy in his eyes!
What weariness without words, what ultimate woe!
And now to-night he stood transfigured here
Clothed in a great serenity and a joy
As if his life had wrought what he would have it.

OGLESBY

Yes, he is changed.   Shall we go on?

                              (*They go out.*)

Scene III.   The entrance of Ford's Theatre.

BOOTH
(*Passing the doorkeeper without a ticket.*)
Is this all right?

DOORKEEPER

                    All right for you.

BOOTH

                    Can you leave,
Go with me for a brandy?

DOORKEEPER

                              No.

BOOTH

Why not?
The play's commenced, and everyone is here.

DOORKEEPER

Not everyone—the presidential party!

BOOTH

They enter without tickets.

DOORKEEPER

Yes, I know.
Go in and watch Miss Keene a little, John.
You might get wakened up to play again,
Marc Antony to your brother's Brutus.

BOOTH

No!
Never with him again. And as for that
My next part will be Brutus.

(*He goes into the theatre.*)

*Scene IV. Lincoln and Mrs. Lincoln Driving to the
Theatre.*

LINCOLN

Mary, the war is over. We have had
Hard times since we came here. But now, thank God,

[144]

BRUTUS LIVES AGAIN IN BOOTH

The war is over.   We may hope for peace,
And happiness for the four years that remain,
While I close up my work as President.
Then back to Illinois to rest and live.
I have some money saved.   Wrote recently
To friends to find a house for me in Chicago—
We can live there, or Springfield.   Law again,
At least enough to keep us.

MRS. LINCOLN

> That's my dream,
And from this night we start to live, rejoice.

(They drive on.)

Scene V.   The stage of Ford's Theatre.
(Laura Keene as "Florence Trenchard"; John Dyatt
as "Dundreary" in dialogue in Tom Taylor's
"American Cousin.")

FLORENCE

"Can't you see the point of that joke?"

DUNDREARY

"No, really."

FLORENCE

"You can't see it?"

DUNDREARY

"No!"

[145]

BRUTUS LIVES AGAIN IN BOOTH

(*Lincoln, Mrs. Lincoln and party enter the box.*)

FLORENCE
(*Making a profound courtesy to Lincoln.*)
"Everyone can see that!"

(*The audience breaks into great applause. The band plays "Hail to the Chief." Lincoln bows to the audience.*)

Scene VI.   Back of the stage.

FIRST STAGE HAND
Whose horse is at the door?

SECOND STAGE HAND
Booth's!

A VOICE
Ten twenty-five.

FIRST STAGE HAND
Ten twenty-five.

SECOND STAGE HAND
Ten twenty-five.

[146]

BRUTUS LIVES AGAIN IN BOOTH

Scene VII.   The Presidential Box.

LINCOLN

Oh, no! No persecution, bloody work,
How to articulate the states again,
Just how to handle the states that left us—well,
There will be problems up from day to day,
During my term, at least.   But no revenge,
No hate, no hanging, killing—rather shoo!
Like Hannah Armstrong used to shoo her chickens.
Let the obstreporous, unreconciled
Go clear to—Halifax—get out! But, Major,
My feeling is to treat the Southern people
As fellow citizens.   To be their fellows
And not their masters is my way.

MAJ. RATHBONE
                                    We need
Your genius, Mr. President, for the work
Of reconstruction more, if that may be,
Then we had need of you to push the war.

MRS. LINCOLN
How do you like the play?

LINCOLN
                          Oh, very good.

BRUTUS LIVES AGAIN IN BOOTH

Scene VIII. Dress Circle.

FIRST AUDITOR
(*Gazing at the Presidential box.*)
What's keeping General Grant?   I came to see
The conqueror of Lee.

SECOND AUDITOR
He will not come.
Too late now.

FIRST AUDITOR
(*Looking at his watch.*)
Yes, ten twenty-five.

SECOND AUDITOR
Who's that?

FIRST AUDITOR
Who?

SECOND AUDITOR
Why, a man as pale as snow
Or ivory, with hair black as a horse's tail
Passed back of the seats there, and approached the
entrance
To Lincoln's box.

FIRST AUDITOR
A secret officer,
With message of a battle.   Oh, perhaps
Sherman has vanquished Johnston!

[148]

BRUTUS LIVES AGAIN IN BOOTH

Scene IX. In the passageway leading to the Presidential box.

BOOTH

Right or wrong, God judge me—never man.
Liberty is dead—I would not live,
Beyond my country's life. Oh, Liberty!
Brutus, sustain me!

Scene X. The Presidential box.

MAJOR RATHBONE
(*Observing Lincoln rise.*)
Can I get something for you?

LINCOLN

I want my coat.
I felt a chill and shudder down my back.
(*He gets his coat and is seated.*)

*Scene XI   Booth at the door of the Presidential box
aiming a pistol.*

BOOTH

Brutus! (*He fires. The President's head falls upon
his breast. Booth rushes into the box, slashes Major
Rathbone with a dagger, leaps from the box to the stage.
Falls, arises.*)

[149]

BRUTUS LIVES AGAIN IN BOOTH

Scene XII.   On the stage.

BOOTH

Sic semper Tyrannis!   The South is avenged!

(*He rushes off.   Great confusion.*)

BOOTH'S PHILIPPI

*(Garrett's Tobacco House, Bowling Green, Virginia,
April 26th, 1865. Booth and Harrold.)*

SCENE I

BOOTH

If this must be, I take it. Be a man.
Don't whine like that. You suffer only from fear.
But if you had this torturing leg. My God!
If you rode sixty miles as I did, flesh
Prodded at every jump by broken bones . . .

HARROLD

What's that?

BOOTH

A dog there in the yard.

HARROLD

Those troopers
We hid from on the way here—Federals—
Did they go on, or follow, hunting us?

BOOTH

We're ended likely. Let us stand our ground.
We have our carbines for the ending up . . .

[151]

BOOTH'S PHILIPPI

But oh, to be thus hunted, like a dog,
Through swamps, woods, thickets, chased by gunboats too,
With every hand against me.   And for what?
For doing what brought honor unto Brutus,
And deathless fame to Tell.   Who'll clear my name?
Who'll print what I have written?   There's the pang
To die and have my spirit and sacrifice
Sealed up in silence, or drowned out in cries
Of "cut-throat" or "assassin."

                              I struck down
A greater tyrant than great Brutus slew.
And my act was more pure than his or Tell's.
One would be great, and one had private wrongs
To heap his country's up for quick revenge.
But I, what greatness could I hope for this?
What wrongs had I except the common wrong?
I struck for country and for that alone;
I struck for liberty that groaned beneath
A tyrant's monstrous tyranny—and now look
The cold hand they extend me in the South
For which I struck!   Our country bleeding, broken,
Cried to me for relief, and I was made
The instrument of God by God alone.

HARROLD

A rooster crows!

BOOTH

                Two hours till morning yet.
It's only two o'clock.

[152]

BOOTH'S PHILIPPI

HARROLD

What shall we do?

BOOTH

To-night we'll try the river once again . . .
Why not return to Washington and end it?
They'd try me and I'd clear my name. Repent?
No, I do not repent. But I've a soul
Too great to die a felon's death. Swift guns
Against a firing wall are honorable.
Before them I can clear my name. O God!
Give me a brave man's death, for I have wronged,
Nor hated no one. And was this a wrong
To kill a tyrant? God must deem it so,
By making it a curse upon our time,
Our country and our countrymen. My fate
How miserable soever it may be
Proves not I did a wrong.

                              Great Milton come
And comfort me in this my agony!
You who could write a tyrant forfeits life
To those whom he oppresses, and 'tis just
To take him off. O curse of Cain no less!
Now I must pray again.

(He prays.)

[153]

BOOTH'S PHILIPPI

SCENE II.   (*At the Garrett House.*)

(*Lieutenant Baker, and a squad, including Boston Corbett.*)

BAKER

(*Knocking at the door.*)   Halloo! halloo!

A VOICE

What's wanted?

BAKER

Open the door!

SCENE III.   (*Inside the Tobacco House.*)

HARROLD

They've come.

BOOTH

Yes! rapping at the door.   Perhaps
Old Garrett will not tell that we are here.
Hold to your carbine.   Do as I command.

SCENE III.   (*At the Garrett House.*)

BAKER

(*Taking Garrett by the throat.*)
Where are these fellows?   In your house?

[154]

BOOTH'S PHILIPPI

GARRETT

No! No!

BAKER

We'll search! Men, search the house!

GARRETT

They are not here!

BAKER

You make yourself accomplice if you hide them.
Last time: where are they?

GARRETT

In the Tobacco House.

SCENE IV. (*Inside the Tobacco House.*)

HARROLD

They're walking toward us.

BOOTH

Do as I command.

BAKER

(*Outside.*)   Come out of there.

BOSTON CORBETT

(*Outside.*)   Lieutenant, they can pick
The whole of us through cracks with their carbines.
Old Garrett says they're armed.

(*He goes back of the tobacco house.*)

[155]

BAKER

> Come out of there.
Five minutes to come out, then I set fire
To the tobacco house.

BOOTH

(*Inside.*)

> Who are you? What do you want?

BAKER

(*Outside.*)
> We want you. And we know you. Come, you are
Booth, assassin of the President. Surrender arms.
Come out!

BOOTH

(*Inside.*)

> I want a little time to think about it.

> (*A silence.*)

BAKER

(*Outside.*)

> Well, now come out.

BOOTH

(*Inside.*)
> You are a brave man, captain, I believe,
Honorable too. I am a cripple, have
One leg, the other broken. Yet no less
If you will take your men a hundred yards
From the door of the tobacco house, I'll come
Out as you command and fight you all.

BOOTH'S PHILIPPI

BAKER

(*Outside.*)

I have not come to fight, but capture you.

BOOTH

(*Inside.*)

Give me a chance for life.   I'll better terms.
If you will take your men off fifty yards
I'll come out, fight you all, till I am killed,
Or kill you all.

BAKER

(*Outside.*)

No!

BOOTH

(*Inside.*)

You are a coward, sir,
Denying to a brave man chance for life.

HARROLD

(*Inside.*)

They've set the house afire!   Now, let me out!
(*The house burns.*)

BOOTH

(*Inside.*)

You hellish coward, would you leave me now?
Go! Go! and leave me.   It would be dishonor
To die with such a coward.
Let this man
Come out of here!

[157]

BOOTH'S PHILIPPI

BAKER

(Outside.)

           All right! Hand out his arms
And come.

BOOTH

(Inside amid flames.)

               A coward goes to cowards.
(The flames are coming up around Booth.)
(He stands on a crutch, pale and defiant.)

SCENE V. *(Boston Corbett looking through a crack in
the Tobacco House at Booth amid the flames.)*

CORBETT

I hear you God and will obey!

    *(He points a carbine through a crack and fires at
    Booth. Booth leaps and falls. The soldiers go in
    and bring him out on the lawn.)*

SCENE VI. *(On the lawn.)*

BAKER

(To Corbett.)

           Why did you shoot? You had no orders to?
I'll take you back to Washington in chains!
Why did you shoot?

[158]

BOOTH'S PHILIPPI

CORBETT
                    God told me to.

BAKER
                    It looks it.
You hit him just behind the ear. Same place
Where Lincoln got the mortal wound.

BOOTH
                    Tell mother
I died for country, liberty, as Brutus
Did what he did for Rome. I thought it best
To do what I have done. God's will be done
As I have tried to do it.

(*He dies.*)

THE BURIAL OF BOSTON CORBETT

(One warden to another.)

(Asylum for the insane, Kansas, 1885.)

So this is what we bury? How his face
Seems like a smear of yellow wax. This beard
Grown fine and curly. Something nasty here,
Hermaphroditic, feminine. Like a dog
That has run loose with rabies, yelps and snaps,
And makes a terror for a day, is slain,
And lies where passers-by can foot the corpse,
So he lies here: this steadfast paranoic!
How vanished from these sealed lids dreams of God!
Where are they now? For all this outer world
Of lunatics, care-takers, wardens, world
Of fields and villages, the state and states
Smiles at these lids so neatly sealed, the God
That had his altar in the spectral light
Of his mad eyes!

                    This is the man who slew
The slayer of the noble Lincoln. First
For the common good was Cæsar slain by Brutus,
And Booth slew Lincoln in a dream of Brutus,
This Corbett slew the slayer in a faith
Of God. Catch up the corner of the sheet.

THE BURIAL OF BOSTON CORBETT

He gets a grave where many hundreds lie,
Each with his epitaph of "Rest in Peace";
Who had no peace in living, for the dreams
Of God, or Duty, Terror, Visions Vain.

Some say he came to Kansas, hither drawn
By hope of sympathy, since all are mad
In Kansas; otherwise the true God know,
And keep His ritual of reform. He found
God mocked in Kansas, or he had not tried
To shoot the state assembly to a man,
When he was keeper of the door. Perhaps
'Twas right enough to slay the actor Booth,
Obeying God; we might accept his word
God told him to kill Booth. But was it God
Commanded him to slay so many honorable
Members of the Kansas legislature
For legislating, or not legislating
As God would have them? Well, I have a doubt.
And many doubted his divine appointment
For massacre like that. And so we flung
The lasso round him, gathered him, and quick
We shut him in the pound, dishonored God,
As he conceived it, doing so.

                                          I've heard
Brutus at last said, Miserable Virtue, Bawd,
Thou wert a world alone, a cheat at last!
This Boston Corbett never did recant
The faith, or God, the word.

THE BURIAL OF BOSTON CORBETT

So ends it here.
Mad unto death! This Corbett is the corneous
And upcurved withered calyx of a flower
Rich out of time. His madness is the lisping
Of that same stricken calyx in the wind
Of Infinite Mysteries.

Are you ready now?
Knot fast your corners of the sheet to hold.
All ready, to the field. There in corruption
We'll sow him, to be raised—but why at all
Should he be raised?

THE NEW APOCRYPHA

BUSINESS REVERSES

(*Mark, Chapter VI.*)

Everything! Counter and scales—
  I'll take whatever you give.
I'm through, and off to Athens,
  Where a man like me can live.

And Hipparch, the baker, is going;
  My chum, who came with me
To follow the crowds who follow
  The prophet of Galilee.

We two were there at Damascus
  Dealing in figs and wine.
Nice little business! Some one
  Said: "Here, I'll give you a line!

"Buy fish, and set up a booth,
  Get a tent and make your bread.
There are thousands who come to listen,
  They are hungry and must be fed."

BUSINESS REVERSES

And so we went. Believe me,
    There were crowds, and hungry, too.
Five thousand stood in the desert
    And listened the whole day through.

Famished? Well, yes. The disciples
    Were saying to send them away
To buy their bread in the village,
    But the prophet went on to say:

"Feed them yourselves, O you
    Of little faith." But they said:
"We have just five little fishes
    And two little loaves of bread."

We heard it, me and Hipparch,
    And rubbed our hands. You see
We were there to make some money
    In the land of Galilee.

We had stock in plenty. We waited.
    I wiped the scales, and my chum
Re-stacked the loaves. We bellowed,
    But no one seemed to come.

"Fresh fish!" I bawled my lungs out:
    "Nice bread!" poor Hipparch cried,
But what did they do? Sat down there
    In fifties, side by side,

BUSINESS REVERSES

In ranks, the whole five thousand.
Then—well, the prophet spoke,
And broke the five little fishes,
And the two little loaves he broke.

And fed the whole five thousand.
Why, yes! So gorged they slept.
And we stood beaten and bankrupt.
Poor Hipparch swore and wept.

They gathered up twelve baskets
Full from the loaves of bread;
Five little fishes—twelve baskets
Of fragments after they fed.

And we—what was there to do
But dump our stock on the sand?
That's what we got for our labor
And thrift, in such a land.

We met a man near Damascus
Who had joined the mystagogues.
He said: "I was wicked as you men
Until I lost my hogs."

Now Hipparch and I are going
To Athens, beautiful, free.
No more adventures for us two
In the land of Galilee.

[165]

THE FIG TREE

(*Matthew, Chapter XXI.*)

With all of the rest of my troubles my fig tree's withered
    and gone.
It stood in the road, you know, I haven't much of a lawn.
I step from my door to a step, and from that right into
    the street.
Just the same I sat under my tree, as a shade from the
    noonday heat.

Camels came by and asses, caravans, footmen, too;
Soldiers of Cæsar saw me and ate of my tree, nor drew
Ax nor sword to the branches, nor even a hack on the
    bole.
Now what had I done or my tree? I call it an evil dole

To a tree that must rest as a man rests. Why last year
    what a crop!
Figs all over the branches, from lower limb to top.
The tree was resting this year, contenting itself with
    leaves,
If magic comes of believing, beware the man who believes.

[166]

THE FIG TREE

If faith can remove a mountain, then faith, I say, beware.
Some morn I'll look toward Olivet and find it no longer
    there.
These fellows can blast our vineyards, level our hills or
    remove.
And what does it prove but faith, what other good does
    it prove?

Nothing at all! Just magic, like Egypt's cunning breed.
And to do such things with faith the size of a mustard
    seed!
What is there need of more? If you gave them faith as a
    pear
They would set Orion dancing around the paws of the
    Bear;

Make the heavens fall on our heads, the whole world
    ruin and wreck;
Slay us and our children, slave us, put the yoke on our
    neck;
Smash cities to strengthen the village, have life just as
    they would.
And make that evil which is not, make evil into a good.

Anyway he came, he was hungry, and it was break of
    dawn.
He ran to my tree expectant, saw nothing but leaves
    thereon.

THE FIG TREE

Then raged for the lack of figs, no grace for the years
   that it bore.
And he said may no fruit grow hereon forevermore.

With that my tree curled up like a leaf in a windy blaze.
I was standing here on my step half blind in a sudden
   maze.
Then he said: have faith and do what I have done to this
   tree,
Or say to the mountains move and be cast into the sea.

So now I have no shade at noon under leafy boughs,
Why the tree was good for resting, cooler than in the
   house,
If it never bore again, if the life is more than meat
Why not this tree for my dreams, though he found no
   figs to eat.

But I swear it had borne next year, it was only taking a
   rest.
There's too many saints who are straining the world to a
   dream in the breast.
Next year no figs for Cæsar, and none for myself, what's
   worse,
If this be the work of faith, then faith itself is a curse.

TRIBUTE MONEY

(Matthew, Chapter XXII:24-27.)

This is all of the story
Capernaum stood in the way,
The takers of tribute came:
"Does your master tribute pay?"

And Peter ran to Jesus,
And Jesus answered him: "Nay!
Do the kings of the earth have tribute
From their own children, pray?

"Or do they get it of strangers?"
And Peter answered him: "Yea."
Then Jesus said: "This is Galilee,
Should Galileans pay?

"But yet lest we offend them
There's a fish out there in the bay
With a silver coin in his mouth—
Go catch the fish and pay."

Did Jesus mean to mock
The tariff laws of the day:
That Peter could catch the fish
As likely as he would pay?

TRIBUTE MONEY

Did he mean to resist or yield
If Peter was lucky that day?
I, Matthew, tell you no more,
And Mark and Luke don't say.

Did we enter the gate, or sit
Where the rocks and olives are gray?
Right then there was better matter
For a follower to portray.

The multitude gathered. He called
A child to him from its play,
And set the child in our midst;
And then he began to say:—

"This is the kingdom of heaven."
And he took its hand and smiled.
"The kingdom of heaven," he said,
"Is like the heart of a child."

And I say, if this be true,
The Kingdom is surely defiled
By laws, and tariffs and kings
Unknown to the heart of a child.

THE GREAT MERGER

(*Exodus, Chapter XX.*)

Philo, the worst has come,
All we foresaw and feared:
Delphos will soon be dumb,
Eleusis felled and cleared.

Not only Marduk and Bel
Shamash, Nana, and Sin
Are doomed to be swallowed.   Rebel?
It is too late to begin.

They have worked for this merger for years;
They have bullied, lied and coerced.
They have played with curses and tears.
And now at last is the worst:

For Zeus goes into the bowl
Of Cyclops, thoroughly blended.
The brew is Jehovah, a Soul
Envious, sour, commended

And forced to our lips.   His son
And another, the Holy Ghost,

[171]

THE GREAT MERGER

Are mixed with him, there is none
Not stirred in the mixture and lost

Of the gods we loved. They say
There is only one god, not many.
Well, who knows, we of clay,
If there be a thousand, or any?

They say there is one—all right!
They take over all the rest.
And so there is one, we can fight,
Argue, pray and protest;

Set up a booth to Apollo,
Athene; bawl and persuade.
The crowds no longer follow—
Jehovah has got the trade.

For the Jews have used the scheme
Of commerce for making a god:
A harbor where no trireme
But their own can dock or load.

Now who will come to dissolve
This theo-monopoly?
And the power they took devolve
On a mightier deity?

It will come. But as for Zeus,
Osiris, Ptah, Zoroaster,

THE GREAT MERGER

They are stewed in the dominant juice
Of Jehovah, lord and master.

We accept the fate. We laugh.
The earth, the sea and the sky
Are at last the cenotaph
Of gods, who always die.

AT DECAPOLIS

(*Mark, Chapter V.*)

I

THE ACCUSATION

I am a farmer and live
Two miles from Decapolis.
Where is the magistrate? Tell me
Where the magistrate is!

Here I had made provision
For children and wife,
And now I have lost my all;
I am ruined for life.

I, a believer, too,
In the synagogues.—
What is the faith to me?
I have lost my hogs.

Two thousand hogs as fine
As ever you saw,
Drowned and choked in the sea—
I want the law!

AT DECAPOLIS

They were feeding upon a hill
When a strolling teacher
Came by and scared my hogs—
They say he's a preacher,

And cures the possessed who haunt
The tombs and bogs.
All right; but why send devils
Into my hogs?

They squealed and grunted and ran
And plunged in the sea.
And the lunatic laughed who was healed,
Of the devils free.

Devils or fright, no matter
A fig or a straw.
Where is the magistrate, tell me—
I want the law!

2

JESUS BEFORE MAGISTRATE AHAZ

Ahaz, there in the seat of judgment, hear,
If you have wit to understand my plea.
Swine-devils are too much for swine, that's clear.
Poor man possessed of such is partly free.

Is neither drowned, destroyed at once, his chains
May pluck while running, howling through the mire

AT DECAPOLIS

And take a little gladness for his pains,
Some fury for unsatisfied desire.

But hogs go mad at once. All this I knew,—
But then this lunatic had rights. You grant
Swine-devils had him in their clutch and drew
His baffled spirit. How significant,

As they were legion and so named! The point
Is, life bewildered, torn in greed and wrath;—
Desire puts a spirit out of joint.
Swine-devils are for swine who have no path.

But man with many lusts, what is his way,
Save in confusion, through accustomed rooms?
He prays for night to come, and for the day
Amid the miry places and the tombs.

But hogs run to the sea. And there's an end.
Would I might cast the swinish demons out
From man forever. Yet the word attend.
The lesson of the thing what soul can doubt?

What is the loss of hogs, if man be saved?
What loss of lands and houses, man being free?
Clothed in his reason sits the man who raved,
Clean and at peace, your honor. Come and see.

Your honor shakes a frowning head. Not loth,
Speaking more plainly, deeper truth to draw;

AT DECAPOLIS

Do your judicial duty, yet I clothe
Free souls with courage to transgress the law.

By casting demons out from self, or those
Like this poor lunatic whom your synagogues
Would leave to battle singly with his woes—
What is a man's soul to a drove of hogs?

Which being lost, men play the hypocrite
And make the owner chief in the affair.
You banish me for witchcraft. I submit.
Work of this kind awaits me everywhere.

And into swine where better they belong,
Casting the swinish devils out of men,
The devils have their place at last, and then
The man is healed who had them—where's the wrong,

Save to the owner? Well, your synagogues
Make the split hoof and chewing of the cud
The test of lawful flesh. Not so are hogs.
This rule has been the statute since the flood.

Ahaz, your judgment has a fatal flaw.
Is it not so with judges first and last—
You break the law to specialize the law?—
This is the devil that from you I cast.

THE SINGLE STANDARD

(St. John, Chapter VIII.)

It was known through Judea, we knew it:—
That Joseph beguiled
By mercy for Mary espoused,
And already with child,

Before they had come to each other,
Would put her away
In secret, before the Sanhedrin
Could summon, array,

The witnesses, judge her and make her
A noise and a shame—
We knew this, and what would he do
If the case were the same

As his father believed was the case
With his mother? would he,
A prophet, fulfill all the law,
Or let her go free?—

This Sarah, you know, that I caught,
Was a witness and saw.
Now what would he do, shade away,
Or judge by the law?

THE SINGLE STANDARD

For Moses decreed if a woman
Who is married shall lie
With a man, whether wedded or not,
The woman shall die

With the man in a volley of stones;
And Moses decreed
If a virgin already betrothed
Shall lust in the deed

With a man not the bridegroom, and whether
The man shall be wed,
The people shall stone them with stones
Until they be dead.

Now mark you, how equal the law
Of weight and of span:
One law for the woman in sin,
The same for the man.

If Moses be still the law-giver,
By nothing dethroned,
And this be the law, then this Sarah
Was fit to be stoned.

And if it be true, as he says,
That he came to fulfill
The law, nor destroy it, why then
We thought he would will

[179]

THE SINGLE STANDARD

The death of this woman we took
In adultery, yes in the act,
So we argued together beforehand
The law and the fact.

Now the case was this way: this Josiah
Late journeyed from Tyre,
Three wives to his household already,
Yet alive with desire,

And free by our custom and law
To add to his hearth
A fourth for the heirs to his house,
And for comfort and mirth,

Came back in the cause of a field
He had bought; as it chanced
Met up with this Sarah, a wife,
They feasted and danced,

Her spouse being absent, what's more
In Egypt for good.
So Josiah and Sarah were found
In the act in the wood.

We brought her before him, accused,
And told him the case.
He stooped, as it seemed, to conceal
A blush on his face,

THE SINGLE STANDARD

And wrote in the sand, as we stood
And pressed him he wrote:
"Anise" and "cummin" and "gnat"
And "Moses" and "mote."

We cried all the more, he uplifted
Himself, said: "Begin
Your throwing of stones, let the first
Be him without sin."

So there I was caught, for he knew—
Like wheat from the scythe
We shrank—I was guilty of sin,
I had failed in my tithe

Of anise. But why have clean hands
To work at our smudges?
And how will you ever stop sin
If you ask of the judges

To be without sin ere they punish
A matter of lust?
I call this a ruling where morals
Fall down in the dust.

The most of us left then. He asked her:
"Does no man condemn?
Nor do I." And so he made one
With me and with them.

THE SINGLE STANDARD

So here in a sense was the world
Spiritual, civil,
Prophet and Pharisee, judge
Leagued up with the devil.

For what did it matter to say
To go and no more
Sin as she had, if the sin
Would fare as before?

It followed that Sarah went free,
And Josiah the man.
One standard for both is the rule,
And the modern plan.

What's that? Why to sin if you wish—
For what is a sin
If no stones are hurled for the lack
Of a man to begin?

And so it all ended. This Sarah
Was given a bill.
She married Josiah, they say,
And lives with him still.

FIRST ENTRANTS

(St. Matthew, Chapter XXII: 31.)

We know the game of lawyer and priest;
We know the cunning of Pharisee, Scribe;
We know the malice of soldier, jailer;—
Hearts of those who abstain, imbibe.

And when we saw a God-mad fool
Like John the Baptist who cursed and grieved
For the hate of the elders, the harlot's sorrow
We listened to him and we believed.

We know we are wronged, he voiced it for us;
We know we are mocked, he gave us place
With the children of grief, the simple hearted,
The broken spirits deserving grace.

He knew men use us and throw us away.
He knew we give and the gift is loathed.
We are the givers to men who scourge us,
Drive us to darkness, cold, unclothed.

And when he said: "Behold he is there
Whose latchet I am unworthy to loose,"
Jesus took us, the humble hearted,
The broken vessels that none will use.

[183]

FIRST ENTRANTS

And we believed again, and saw
A youth who loved us without desire;
Feasting, drinking with us the harlots,
Outcasts, sinners, wrecks of the fire.

These were our brothers: John the Baptist,
Jesus of Nazareth. Brothers I say.
Brothers and sisters bound in the service
Of giving comfort and pity away.

Pity and solace and hope of heaven,
Healing and tenderness came of Christ.
And we, the harlots, have given pity
And given delight to men who enticed

This little gift, so easy to give;
This wonder gift to them, as they said.
That is the passion that moves a woman
Before it becomes a matter of bread.

Before the lashes of scorn and the chains,
The dungeons, before the scowls and sneers;
Before the wrath of the priest, the temple's
Bolted door for our hunger, tears.

Before the delight we sell is stale
As the steps of a dancer, growing old.
All is delight, kisses and dancing—
Men can buy, for they have the gold.

FIRST ENTRANTS

And we, he says, shall enter heaven
Before the priests and the elders do.
Why do we enter? Because as sorrow,
Poverty, humbleness, we are true.

Without pretense or pride. We are children
Who have shirked the task, but repent the sin.
But they, the elders and priests have promised
To work for heaven and never begin.

Why do we enter, save spite of our craft
To wheedle with lies we all stand forth
Known to the world as painted harlots,
Taken by no one over our worth?

And it's good to enter, if we can be
With Jesus and John, and given reprieve
From priests and elders who run the city
And hound the harlots who see and believe.

JOHN IN PRISON

(*St. Luke, Chapter XVI.   St. Matthew, Chapter XI.*)

John said to the jailer: "Where are my disciples? Be-
    friend
My grief and my doubt, and entreat them to come, to the
    end

That they ask him for me if we look for another, or
    deem,
As I did, that this prophet shall save and fulfill and
    redeem."

And the jailer replied: "Since the wrath of King Herod
    a dish
Your head shall contain by to-morrow, I give you your
    wish."

So he brought the disciples to John and the two of them
    led
To the cell where he sat, and John to the two of them
    said:—

JOHN IN PRISON

"At this end of my life and my hopes, at the door of my
    doom
Go ask him for me and report: is it he that should come,

Or shall we yet look for another?"   Amazed were the
    two
And one of them spoke to the Baptist and said: "Is it true

That you preached in the wilderness saying repent and
    prepare
The way of the Lord, whose shoes I am worthless to bear;

Who will fan out the chaff, gather wheat, purge the floor
With fire and the Spirit baptize you, bring down and
    restore

The kingdom of heaven?   And are we abused in the word
That as he came out of the waters of Jordan you heard

A voice call from heaven which thundered: 'This son of
    my love
With whom I am pleased you shall hear,' and a dove

For the Spirit descended upon him—and yet can you ask
If he be the one that should come?   Yet we take up the
    task

And go at your bidding."   And John said: "I suffer
    without
You seek him and ask, for this is the cause of my doubt:—

[187]

JOHN IN PRISON

I have heard of his works and rejoice. But why does he
    feast
When I fasted myself? And how have the rumors in-
    creased

That he fellows with publicans, sinners and drinkers of
    wine,
A bibber himself, when the springs of the desert were
    mine?

And how is the ax, as I said, laid close to the root of the
    tree,
And my curses fulfilled of the Pharisees, if this must be?

And if, as they say, he is preaching the word that we make
Of the unrighteous mammon a friend for the day when
    we break

With the lords of the riches of truth, as he put it, for then
The unrighteous mammon shall take us, console us
    again:—

I have wasted the goods of my lord! I am caught and
    accused!
Shall I make good the theft from my lord in a trust I
    abused?

Why, no! I go out to the debtors, my master to foil,
How much do you owe him? Why, so many measures of
    oil!

JOHN IN PRISON

Sit down then, I say, make the bill but a half, quickly
    write:—
I am wiser in this, so he says, than the children of light—

As I make for myself by the trick of a thief, and a theft,
The confederates' home for my own for my honor bereft.

Go! learn if he said this.   Return ere the rise of the
    sun:—
Shall we look for another to save us, or is he the one?"

ANANIAS AND SAPPHIRA

Who is that coming? Look! They are bearing a body
    again.
It's a woman now, I think. And the very same young
    men

Who brought Ananias' body we buried a moment ago.
Pat down the earth a little, the grass will sooner grow.

Yes, now I see it's Sapphira. What did she do to win
Death at the hands of Peter, or was it her husband's sin?

To which she agreed, or kept her husband's secret in faith.
They sold a sheep, as I hear it, and suffered sudden death

For hiding part of the price, for a thing commendable:
Their boy is sick, and they needed money to get him well.

Just look how things are going: Cæsar the despot rules,
The state is his. For the rest, we are run by a pack of
    fools;

Zealots and mystics who say that the end of the world is
    near.
Tyranny around us, on top, under us dullness and fear.

ANANIAS AND SAPPHIRA

Songs and the wine-cup banished, freedom throttled blue.
It's the same here being a Greek, Persian, Median, Jew.

Roman sovereignty over us, merciless, cold and bright.
Fogs over the land of dust, day no different than night.

Listless we labor or idle, creep into an early bed.
Sleep is the best thing now, and the best is the sleep of the
    dead.

Prepare for the end of the world! Build up the church,
    the throne,
Sell all your goods and give, have nothing to call your
    own;

Put everything in common. That's one cry. What re-
    mains?
Taxes, soldiers, prisons, edicts, laws and chains.

There never was such a time! What man is lord of his
    soul?
Someone entered my barn and took my ass with foal

For the prophet to ride on in triumph. I was there and
    saw him ride,
Crowds crying hallelujah pressing on every side.

They would have all things in common. They kill a man
    and his wife,
And Cæsar rules as always, and yet they call this life!

ANANIAS AND SAPPHIRA

Wars forever and ever, manned by hovels and huts;
And what is it all about? lands, and gold and guts;

And baptists stirring the dreamers, and bankers that
thrive thereby.
Why kill off Ananias when the whole of life is a lie?

All right, young men, put her down. Go to it now with
the spade.
We'll bury the woman Sapphira here where her husband's
laid.

They're out of it. Neither Cæsar nor Peter can wake
their sleep.
I lost my ass, and they lost their lives for the price of a
sheep.

And Cæsar will rule forever! And Peter if he grows
strong
Will make a pact with Cæsar, and Israel's woe and wrong

Will spread all over the earth. It takes no prophet to see
That while there is Gold and Fear man will never be
free—

Until the world is fed, and hunger steals like a wraith
With the ghost of Cæsar's lust, and the mist of Peter's
faith.

THE TWO MALEFACTORS

Ask Matthew, or ask Mark, and get the truth.
I know myself, was there and heard them both—
Both railed at him. No! one did not rebuke
The other for his railing; did not ask
To be remembered when into his Kingdom
Jesus should come. What kingdom? David's?—pah!
That had gone whirling with the desert's dust.
What kingdom? That within you? A fool's kingdom!
"To-day thou shalt be with me in Paradise,"
He never said that. I was there. I know.
And if he did, where is that paradise?
Where is he? And where is the man they say
He said this to? Ask Matthew, learn the truth:
Both railed at him. Both died, nerved to the last
By bitter disappointment.

              Listen, friend,
These malefactors were my brothers! Well,
I saw them grow up lusty. I beheld
Their course from hope to action, till defeat
And prison took them.

              For we are the sons,
We Jews, of those who went to Babylon;

THE TWO MALEFACTORS

Returned to fall by Alexander's sword;
Were snatched by Syria, then Egypt came,
Put heels upon our necks. Rome sailed to us,
And took us over. And these bitter years
Made poets, prophets of us, spurred us on
To inflate the dream Jehovah with our breath
Of threats and curses; yet these bitter years
Kept at white heat the hope of David's throne,
Restored, triumphant, and our prophecies
Were from Jehovah of a king to come
Who would free Israel, drive the oppressor off,
And let us live as men.

                    Now it may be
A certain Jacob was his grandfather,
As Matthew says; or it may be that Heli
Was his grandfather, as Luke says, but still
Both say he was of David. And Luke says
The angel Gabriel came to Mary, his mother,
And said he shall be great and shall be called
The Son of the Most High, and God shall give him
The throne of his father David. He shall reign
Over the house of Jacob, and his kingdom
Shall have no end. We looked for such a one
To free us and with portents such as stars,
And Gabriel descending, Bethlehem
Become his birth-place, and the prophecies
Of old fulfilled, we looked for Israel freed,
And for a king of Jewish blood to rule us—

THE TWO MALEFACTORS

No Cæsar any more. For it was prophesied
Of Bethlehem: For out of thee shall come
A governor, a shepherd of my people!
And look, he's born in Bethlehem! And why not
Our hope re-kindled?

              And now look at us;
These centuries bruised, imprisoned and made poor,
Jerusalem a city of wails and woes,
The whole of Israel slaved! And look at him!
How does he start his work, whatever it be?
By reading from Isaiah at Nazareth:—
"The spirit of the Lord is upon me, because
He anointed me to preach good tidings to
The poor, hath sent me to proclaim release
To captives and to set at liberty
Them that are bruised."

              What doctrine may this be,
But change, or revolution, and the ferment
Of new wine bursting bottles frail and old,
This tyranny of Cæsar, this dependence
On alien rulership? You know yourself
Barabbas was not single in the crime
Of insurrection, ask the fellow Mark.
He'll tell you this Barabbas lay in bonds
With many who rose up, committed murder.
Of these were my two brothers, crucified
With Jesus on that day.

[195]

THE TWO MALEFACTORS

                    Well, so it was
He preached, was followed by the poor, the weak,
The slaved, despoiled until 'twas noised abroad
Through all the hill country and in the cities
That he stirred up the people everywhere,
Devising revolution, overthrow
Of Cæsar's rule. But there was murmuring too:
For some said he was good, and others said
He deceived the people. For upon a day
When he was asked directly of our tribute,
Whether to pay to Cæsar, not to pay,
He dodged and said: "Give Cæsar his due and God
His due"; but what we wished to know, was what
Was Cæsar's due, and give it him, and if
No tribute was his due, but rather casting
The yoke of Cæsar, then give Cæsar that.
He did not answer what the Pharisees asked,
That which *we* wished to hear him answer, though
The Pharisees had asked him. For we poor,
Enslaved and disinherited had followed
His leadership thus far.

                    Behold the change:
Passing from work unfinished he becomes
The Son of God and God himself, becomes
A mystery, the Word that lived and wrought
Before John who announced him. Tidings preached,
I grant you, to the poor, but who remain
Poor as before, but worn for broken hope

THE TWO MALEFACTORS

Of words that changed no thing. And no release
To captives, and no liberty to those
Bruised and in chains. And so I say his work
Is left unfinished, nothing done in truth.
And quickly, like a sun-rise on the hills,
He flashes forth his God-head, and we're left
To Cæsar's will, and end up with the words:—
His kingdom is of heaven, not of earth;
Refines the point: this kingdom is within us.
And he will die and rise again from death,
Ascend to heaven, and return again
Before this generation passes to take up
His own to heaven, and will rule forever
In heaven, not in Israel. For the world
Is to be burnt, with all its disbelievers.
And when it's burnt, sitting at God's right hand
He'll rule forever with his own! You see
What we expected vanished in such words,
Such madness, idle dreams.

                         But, as I said,
His lineage was David's; Matthew, Mark
Will tell you so. But David said of Christ,
Calling him Lord; sit thou on my right hand
Till I make enemies of thine thy foot-stool.
"How is Christ son of David, being his Lord?"
Asked Jesus of the Pharisees, closed their mouths
With asking that. The common people heard
Him gladly when he said this—true enough!

THE TWO MALEFACTORS

But I, my brothers, did not hear him gladly.
For if he were the son of God, yet equal
In being and in time with God, why not
The son and lord of David? Both perplex
The spirit of man; one mystery is as dark
As another mystery, and if one be so, then
Another may be also. Pass the point. . . .

They crucified my brothers with him! Both
Railed on him for deliverance from the cross.
If he were God, he could have plucked the nails
And let them down, escape. And listen now:
My brothers kept their faith in him to the last,
And since they were condemned and had to pay
For insurrection on the cross, chose out
His day of crucifixion for their own;
Believed that he would save them, and so make
This choosing of his time of penalty
An hour of luck. And so I tell you truth:
Though both were railing it was rather pain
Than lack of hope that made them rail at him.
Nor was it mockery that made them rail.
They hoped to stir him by their words, evoke
His greatest strength to help them that they railed.
They even smiled a little when the nails
Were driven through their hands, as if to say:
"You cannot harm us when this god is here;
Go, do your butcher business, for at last
He'll save himself and us." And just as men

THE TWO MALEFACTORS

Refuse to think death near, and still believe
They will escape it somehow, when no aid,
But human hands is near, my brothers thought
This god would surely save them. So they talked,
Hunched up their legs and shoulders to ease up
The strain of hanging on the nails, and waited,
Joked with the lookers on, and smiled and begged,
And sweated agony and railed at last.
But when the voices in the crowd called out:
"If you trust God, let God deliver you,
If you are God's son, let Him save you now;
Save thou thyself!" my older brother said:
"If I were off this cross I'd break your heads,
You crooked priests, you whited sepulchers,
You carrion Scribes and Pharisees."

                           And such noise
As they cast lots to get his garments, shouts
When they were won and parted! In a silence
He asked his Father to forgive them, saying
They knew not what they did. My brother bawled:
"They know what they are doing, they have killed
The prophets in all ages! Don't say that!
Don't end up soft, you cursed them hitherto,
These are the vipers that you cursed before;
These are the vultures that you said you'd shut
The gates of heaven against; these are the wolves
That thirst for blood and lap it, unrepentant
Blasphemers against you and the Holy Ghost;

THE TWO MALEFACTORS

Committers of unpardonable sins, the band
You drove with knotted cords from out the temple.
And what is usury or selling doves
To killing you? Why ask your Father this?
Why now this softness? Change of mood, why prayers
Instead of curses? If you're dying, sire,
Be what you were when you were flush with life,
And curse them into hell. Hold to your strength,
And curse them into hell." And so it went
With talking back and forth, mixed in with groans,
And curses, railings, while my brothers twisted
Their bodies, and hunched up their thighs and backs
To ease the strain of hanging on the nails,
And dribbled at the mouth, and babbled things
And laughed like devils in a soul possessed.

But when he thirsted and they took a sponge
And gave him vinegar, and he sucked it in,
They looked at him with eyes that bulged with fear:—
They saw him drooping, fainting, losing strength,
They struggled then and shouted: "Keep on breathing!
Breathe deep! Call on your Father! Don't give up!
Fight for your life, your god-head and ourselves!
We're here because you came and preached, and stirred
The people! Don't desert us now! Great Lord,
Messiah, Son of God, are we first martyrs
To what you failed to do? We cannot die,
You must not die. Let David's throne be lost
As lost it is, but not our lives! Great Lord!"

THE TWO MALEFACTORS

Thus as they chattered, chattered, bawled and shouted
Jesus threw back his head and cried so loud
That all the valleys echoed it: "My God,
My God, why hast thou forsaken me?" And then
His head dropped on his chest—and he was dead. . . .

They looked at him—my brothers looked at him,
And whimpered—they were beaten, but fought on.
Tears stained with blood went coursing down their cheeks.
And then the soldiers came to break their legs.
And one had fainted, but the other one
Was fighting still and said: "Have mercy friend,
Cæsar would save me, what does Cæsar care
For one poor rebel?"

          Then they broke their legs,
And all were dead. So ended up another
Chapter in this poor world's hopeless hope.

BERENICE

AGRIPPA
How is it with this people?

FESTUS
     Much the same.
They kick the Roman rule. Like flame in stubble,
Which being slapped with sticks, leaps up and spreads,
Oppression makes them hotter.

BERENICE
       And why not?
Seeing their customs, altars, arks and temples
The beauty of their faith, as they have dreamed it,
And fashioned it with hands from gold and wood
Is desecrated.

FESTUS
      How to firmly keep
The rule of Cæsar, leave their god untouched,
That is the problem. Where the state and god
Are one, inseparable, can Cæsar rule
And not subject their god? There was this Judas
Together with a Pharisee named Sadduk
Who fought the Roman census of the Jews,

[202]

BERENICE

Raised revolution in religion's name,
A cunning strategy. You could not crush
The revolution, leave their faith unharmed.
And now this new sect called the Nazarenes—
The country's in a tumult.

AGRIPPA
                    Yes, these Nazarenes,
The worst of all.

BERENICE
                    I have heard the desert
Fosters a little burr of poisonous spines
Which sometimes as the lion roams the sands,
Sticks in the hairy clefts between his claws.
It itches, stings, and maddens; with a growl
The lion lays him down and with his tongue
Licks out the pest. It sticks upon his tongue.
He has no second tongue to lick it thence.
It sticks and stings. The poison spreads apace
And puffs the rebelling member till his throat
Narrows for breath. And then he runs and roars,
And with his nose plows through the sand, lies down,
Digs in the desert, leaps, rolls over, froths,
Grows green of eye; chokes to his death at last.
Rome is your lion, and the burr these Jews.

AGRIPPA
Sweet sister, be as apt with counsel as
Your parable is apt.

[203]

BERENICE

BERENICE

> You have my word.
Let them alone, their internecine strife
'Twixt sect and sect fight out. Madmen they are
And zealots—let them choke and strive and wail.
Jesus they killed and Stephen. But should Rome
Repress religions, doctrines, script or speech?
If what they teach be false 'twill die, if true
You cannot kill it.

AGRIPPA

> You could say as well
If thickets bear no apples they will die;
If they bear apples you can kill them not.
But thickets bear no apples. Apple trees
Fall easily to the ax. And so with truth,
And false truth. Where you have one man who's wise
You have a million fools, who take the stones
Of ignorance and error in their hands
And overwhelm the wise. Rome shall not fall,
Recede, relent before a mob like this.

FESTUS

They seem to thrive by being mowed, and yet
If left uncut they choke us. There is Paul,
My heritage from Felix, jailed two years,
And brought before me by the Jews, who charged
Offenses numerous against him, such
As breaches of the Jewish law, attacks
Upon their temple, on the emperor,

BERENICE

Contemned perhaps, the which they could not prove.
Now to report to you, O King, my judgment
Divided in the case of Paul. I sought
To do the Jews a pleasure. So I asked:
Will you go to Jerusalem and be judged?
But Paul replied: I stand at Cæsar's seat,
There should my judgment be.

AGRIPPA

                    O, wicked Rome,
Whose laws become a haven to her foes
When they are troubled.

FESTUS

                 Yes, I told these Jews
Rome does not give a man to die before
He meets his accusers face to face, has time
To answer for himself. And so it was
I came to Cæsarea, had him brought
And heard the case. As I supposed, they charged
This Paul with nothing, only matters raised
Of their own superstitions, and of Jesus
Whom Paul affirmed, affirms to be alive,
Though dead long since. But as he had appealed
To Cæsar I commanded he be kept
Till I might send him. But what shall I say?
How shall I send him, after all, to Cæsar
Without a writing that shall signify
Why and for what I send him? Cæsar's time
Is not for crimeless causes.

BERENICE

AGRIPPA

Nevertheless
As he's appealed to Cæsar he must go.
But I would hear him.

FESTUS

I have sent for him
That you may hear him. There, he enters now!
(*Paul is brought in.*)
He has a speech that he has often made
How first he persecuted, for in truth Agrippa
He is a catapult that has sprung up
As far as he was pulled the other way.
And he will tell you how he stoned this Stephen,
And hunted Nazarenes: and how he went
With writs of persecution from the priests
Up to Damascus, on the way saw light
From heaven, heard the voice of Jesus cry
That he should be a minister to the faith,
And preach as he had persecuted. You see
The rebound of nature, mind.

BERENICE

How thin,
How pale he is, how bright his eyes! Agrippa
Confine him to the matter of this god
Who died, and from the dead arose. O Death,
You are man's horror, and we brood upon you,
Our altars are placations to your wrath.
This Paul is mad for thinking of you, mad

[206]

BERENICE

With faith that he has conquered you.   Look there!
See how his eyes are staring bright as fire—
I am afraid.   And yet if it were true
Jesus arose, nay if the world could be
Persuaded that he rose, the faith would sweep
The world with fire, and crumble every temple
And altar of our gods in almighty Rome.
Look how he stares!

AGRIPPA

There is a noble madness,
A madness which has slaved nobility
And energy and eloquence.   Say now
Who saw this Jesus after he arose?
Did Paul?   Who saw him?

FESTUS

No one that I know.
Not Paul.   He says a multitude.   Some disciples,
Some women, and one Peter.

AGRIPPA

Where are they?
Bring one to me.   Bring Peter; bring a woman.
This is the cause I'd hear.   And if this Paul
Can bring me witness, though his crime were great
As Hannibal's on Rome, I'll set him free.
Why look at him!   Is this new matter to me?
Is he the first who for the gods went mad?

[207]

BERENICE

Or for the mystery of life went mad?
Or madness took for what we are and why,
And what this life means?   For this world has seen
A perfect harmony and working thought
And inspiration in a thousand minds
Of madness on some matter.   Fellow, come
Close here before me.   Look at me.   Yes, well,
There is the light of rising suns, and stars
That burn immortally, in your eyes.   Now speak.
Did Jesus die?

PAUL

He died.

AGRIPPA

Did he arise?

PAUL

He arose.

AGRIPPA

How long being dead?

PAUL

Three days.

AGRIPPA

Saw you him in life?

PAUL

No.

[208]

BERENICE

AGRIPPA

In death?

PAUL

No.

AGRIPPA

After he rose?

PAUL

No! I only heard his voice.

AGRIPPA

Where?

PAUL

On the way to Damascus.

AGRIPPA

What did he say?

PAUL

"It is hard for thee to kick against the pricks."

AGRIPPA

What else?

PAUL

I asked, "Who art thou Lord?"

AGRIPPA

And then?

[209]

BERENICE

PAUL

"I am Jesus," he said, "whom thou persecutest.
To thee have I come to make of thee a witness
And a minister."

AGRIPPA

Since then you have preached,
For which the Jews have persecuted you
As you stoned Stephen?

PAUL

Yes.

AGRIPPA

And you affirm
That Jesus from the dead arose?

PAUL

Thou hast said.
But also I affirm that all shall rise
From death who in the Christ believe, save those
Who live now, and shall die not ere he come.

AGRIPPA

He comes again?

PAUL

Quickly, even before
This generation passes.

[210]

BERENICE

AGRIPPA

You are mad.
Do you appeal to Cæsar?

PAUL

I appeal.

AGRIPPA

Why not be stoned as Stephen was and rise?
If you believe in Jesus, you believe
They cannot kill you.

PAUL

As you will, O King.
I must finish my course, whatever time I die.

AGRIPPA

I could have set you free, if you had taken
To Cæsar no appeal.   Being as it is
I send you up to Rome.   Who can find out
The workings of a mind?   Yet true it is
He saves himself out of a cunning thought
Of this appeal to Cæsar.   Turn him over
To the Centurion Julius—on to Rome.
We have conferred together.   He has done
No thing deserving death.   Take him to Rome.
He'll find a house and hire it, in Rome
Live unmolested, preach, hear Mithra preached
Who cheated death, they say, as Jesus did.
Now let us rise and to the banquet room.
Come Sister, Festus, to the banquet room.

NEBUCHADNEZZAR: *OR* EATING GRASS

Nebuchadnezzar the King, called Ha-Rashang,
Which is to say, the wicked, by the Jews;
I, King of Babylon, the beautiful,
The mighty who have spread the prospering code
Of Hammumrapi, and the obelisk
Of diorite whereon the code is stamped,
Kept in the Temple of Marduk, myself
The lover of progress, beauty, breathe this prayer:
Peace to all peoples, nations, languages
That dwell in all the earth, and also peace
Be multiplied to you; this I record
Upon these bricks of Babylon, and as well
My glory and my madness.

                   First attend:
What would the gods, the god Jehovah even
Have me to do, me gifted with this strength,
This wisdom, skill in arms?   Sit in a hut
Of mud beside the Tigris, be a marsh
Of spirit, sleeping, oozing, grown with flags?
Or be Euphrates rushing, giving life
And drink of life to fields?   What should I do?
Suffer this Syra to dream and drool?

NEBUCHADNEZZAR: *OR* EATING GRASS

Jerusalem to boast, dispute and trade,
And vaunt its favoring heaven, or go forth
And smite Jerusalem and Tyre and take them,
And lead their peoples back to Babylon,
And make them work and serve me, build canals,
Great reservoirs, my palace, city walls,
The Hanging Gardens, till my Babylon
In all this would become a wonder, terror
And worthy of my spirit, hope and dream;
A city and a kingdom in the world
Become the external substance, form and beauty,
Administration, order of a soul
Lordly and gifted—mine, my Babylon,
My dream expressed!

That which I did they tried
To do and failed in doing, even themselves
Would rule as I have ruled, build as I builded,
Win glory as I won it; to that end
Did they invoke their gods, and in the mouths
Of gods and of Jehovah put the curses
And wails of failure. I have triumphed, now
My gods are full of song; I have maintained
My kingdom and my spirit, driving out
The aggressor Necho, who came forth from Egypt,
Syria and Palestine to take from me,
Him I destroyed at Carchemish—my spirit
Have I regained and healed. And now in age,
These eighty years of life gone over me,

NEBUCHADNEZZAR: *OR* EATING GRASS

And rulership of forty years, I sit
Within the level sun-light of my age,
And at this close of day upon my roof
And view my Babylon; but without fear
Madness will come upon me ever again.
The glory of my kingdom has returned,
My honor and my brightness have returned;
My counselors and lords have come to me;
I am established in my age, and excellent
Majesty is added unto me.

All this
Though here upon this roof, upon this spot,
My madness came upon me, when I looked
Over the roofs and temples of my city
And said: Is not this Babylon, the great,
That I have builded for my kingdom's house
By the might of my power and for the honor
Of my great majesty?   Why was it so?

First genius and the dream, then toil and pain
While hands lay stone on stone, and as the stones
Rise from the earth, where naked slaves cry out,
Wheel, lift and grunt; and mortar, scaffolding,
Pillars of cedar strewn confusedly,
Your dream is blurred, even while your city rises
Out of the dream.   I was like to a woman
In the pain of travail, who is mad with pain,
Scarce knows her friends or what is being done,

[214]

NEBUCHADNEZZAR: *OR* EATING GRASS

Nor needs to know, since nature orders all,
Delivers her, but lets the mid-wife lift
The infant to her breast.   Even so with me,
I had conceived this Babylon, nourished it
In the womb of my genius where it grew, came forth
Whole like a child at last from scaffoldings,
Confusion, waste of mortar, stone and bronze.
And when it was accomplished, then my madness
Came on me in a moment of clear seeing
That this which was within me, was without me;
Was substance and reality before me;
Was even myself gone out of me, as the child
Goes from the mother—then my madness came
Not when I saw it first, for I had seen it
Both from this roof and from the Hanging Gardens,
And from the temple of Bel, and in the streets;
But seen it without knowing, as the mother
Exhausted, dulled with agony may know
The child is born, without the consciousness,
The wonder and the rapture of the child,
As the miracle that was of her, but now
Is a miracle external and a life,
A beauty separate, that walks from her
And has its life and way, herself and hers,
But different and its own.
                                    And so it was
When I beheld my Babylon, saw my dream
Spread out before me, clear and definite,
A beauty separate, my very soul

NEBUCHADNEZZAR: *OR* EATING GRASS

Torn out of me and fashioned into stone,
Having its life and way, myself and mine,
Yet being itself, its own. If I had seen
Myself divided and become two men,
My other self come toward me, stand, extend
His hand to me, my terror were not more
Than this to see my Babylon. In that moment
My madness came upon me.

                              But before,
Some nights and days before this I had lain
In troubled dreams upon my couch, had dreamed
Of images and trees, for daily cares
Of empire and the fears of change and loss
Had entered in my dreams. Cyaxeres
Dreamed that a vine grew from his daughter's womb
And overshadowed Asia, which denoted
Her offspring should be clothed with majesty
And rulership of Asia. As for me,
My tree was felled, only the stump was left,
Bound to the earth with brass and iron—this
Foretold what I am now, as Daniel said,
Interpreting my dream. These dreams had come
Which shook me for the thought of human life—
How frail and fleeting! But again to hear
Curses about me for my work and genius
Called by these Jews Ha-Rashang; and to feel
Though I had chosen Daniel, Hananiah,
Michael, Azariah for mine own,
And to be taught to help me in the task

NEBUCHADNEZZAR: *OR* EATING GRASS

Of my administration; even though
I chose all men for duty, wisest use
And in my great humanity and strength
Had placed my subjects where they best could serve
The beauty and the progress of my city—
Though, as I said, to feel that I had done
All things for good and with no thought but good,
Yet still to hear these curses and to see
The worthlessness of human kind, the crowd,
I bowed my head and prayed to Ishtar saying:
Make me an animal and let me feed
With beasts instead of these: So had I prayed
Before my madness in that moment came.

Then as to that, my madness: it was sunset,
I walked upon my palace's level roof,
And looked upon my Babylon; then I thought
Of all my labors, how I had restored
The temples of Borsippa, Uruk, Ur,
Sippar and Larsa, Dilbat; made the plains
Below the great Euphrates rich in corn;
Brought plenty to my people, bread and wine
To all my people; laughter, as it may be,
Between our fated tears to all my people,
And then I looked on Babylon lying there
Beneath the evening's sunlight, safe behind
Its sixty miles of walls unscalable,
Rising four hundred feet, impregnable
For near a hundred feet of width in stone.

NEBUCHADNEZZAR: *OR* EATING GRASS

I saw its hundred gates of durable bronze;
My eyes were lifted to the terraces
Up, up above the river to the temple
Of Bel who blessed my city, and I saw
The temples built to Nebo, Sin and Nana,
Marduk and Shamash, saw my aqueducts,
The houses of my people, in between
The palm grooves and the gardens bearing food
Enough to feed the city if besieged;
Beheld the Hanging Gardens which I built
To soothe Amytis, who had memories
Of mountainous Media, gazing on
The Babylonian plains.

              So as I stood
And looked upon my city, voices passed
Below me muttering Ha-Rashang, and then
This Babylon, my Babylon, lay before me
As my genius realized, grown out of me,
Myself become another, and a being
Which once was me, but now no more was me,
Was mine and was not mine; and with that thought
Rising like Enlil, god of storm and thunder,
Over my terrored spirit, I grew mad
And fled among the beasts, where for a season
I ate grass with the oxen, let the dew
Fall on my body, till my hairs were grown
Like eagle's feathers and my nails were grown
Like claws of birds.   In madness and in hate
Of men and life, in loathing of my glory,

NEBUCHADNEZZAR: *OR* EATING GRASS

My genius and my labors did I live;
In loathing of these tribes who hate the mother
Goddess of our ritual and belief:
Tribes who have made religion of the hate
Of procreative nature, curse the flame
Of beauty, and of love wherewith I built
This Babylon of glory, lust of life;
Till nature cured me and I came again
To rule my Babylon, my excellence
Of majesty returned.

               What am I now,
Bowed with these eighty years? My Babylon,
What is it now to me? I am a father
Whose son is aging, even has made his place
And lived to see it fade, diminish. A son
So old his sonship is a memory,
Has almost ceased to be—that's Babylon.
And I, the father, know this Babylon
As creature of my loins, yet indeed
This city scarcely differs from the cities
That lie afar, as aging sons are men
Among the men of earth, but scarcely more
To a father bent with time than other men.
For in my riotous genius, like a vine
I did put forth this branch, the vine decays,
The branch will live a season. Out of genius
And lust of life to madness, out of madness
To this tranquillity, and this setting sun,
This peace with heaven.

HIP LUNG *ON* YUAN CHANG

You like store? You like Chinese tea? You like me?
You like silk, fan, screen, dragon, pearl chair, jade;
You like Chinese tobacco, picture, Budda too,
Well, as Geesu Klist? All light Lee,
You Chinaman, maybe. I like Chicago too.
I like you, and Hinky Dink, lots I like.
Good city here, much friends. I make some money,
Go back to China sometime. Keep store here,
Come back to store.

                   China old country, vely old country,
Wise country, much wise men long time ago.
Here book Shu Ching, about old time,
More'n tree tousand year ago. Here Lun Yu book
About Confucius, live long time ago, much time
Before live Geesu; taught love one another,
Be good to good men; bad men be fair to; speak truth.
Where sun and moon shine, all place, love and honor
Come to Confucius, brother of God.

                           More yet:
Lao Tzu great man, too, who say be good
To bad men; Chinaman read; close book and speak
What book says; to be wise, Chinese learn to speak

HIP LUNG *ON* YUAN CHANG

What book say closed, on shelf, burned up, or lost.
Chicago good town, Amelika good country, England,
Europe good country too, but China good country,
Wise long time ago, when no Amelika was,
No town in England, and no book in Europe,
Two tousand year before Geesu Kliste came.
Some say Budda greater than Kliste;
Chinee say Confucius greater than Budda.
I say all gods; leave alone—what you care?
Kill Chinaman if you wish, golden rule is golden rule
In Pekin, or Jerusalem.

                    Geesu Kliste people,
Salvation Army come and say: "Hip Lung,
Be saved, love Geesu Kliste, be baptized."
I know the Four Books, I say the Four Books
And never look; but when I say Confucius
Taught Golden Rule and love, they say, not clear
Like Geesu Kliste, Confucius heathen man,
Not good like Geesu Kliste. All light! All light!
I sing about the Dragon Boats, go round
The store till they go on. They no read
The Four Books, no care. Sometime I ask
Why China not hear about Geesu Kliste for years.
Why? Eh? We hear of Budda, why
No hear of Kliste?

               Kliste people say
Tree hundred year they know Kliste comin'—
China no hear. China hear 'bout Budda

HIP LUNG *ON* YUAN CHANG

Tree hundred year after Budda die.
Ming Ti, great king, sent down India
To hear 'bout God Budda.
China no hear of Kliste then . . .
Tousand year after God Budda die,
Great man come to China; Fa Hsien,
Kliste dead now four hundred year,
But China no hear. Why?
Fa Hsien go to India to get books about Budda.
Go trou Gobi desert—no birds, tigers,
But much dragons and devils.
Fa Hsien go to Benares, Budda, Gaya, Ceylon
Come back with books about light way;
See light, hope light, speak light,
Do light, live light, try light; light mind,
Light happiness. And China hear
And love Budda! . . .

Kliste dead four hundred year—
Alle time much people in China, temples, cities,
Much books, many wise men.
And Kliste dead now six hundred year,
And China no hear. Kliste!
Same time god Budda grow in China.

Kliste dead more'n six hundred year,
And Arabs come from Medina to Canton,
Tell about prophet of God Muhammed—Allah!
But no Kliste much.

[222]

HIP LUNG *ON* YUAN CHANG

Next year, Kliste dead now 'bout 630 year.
Salvation Army come from Persia, and China hear
'Bout Kliste, too late; god Budda worshipped now
By much China people.

Year before Salvation Army from Persia
Great man come again: Yuan Chang.
He go to India to get books
'Bout god Budda, and see holy place.
You no hear 'bout Yuan Chang?   No?
Greek men, great men, and Cheeser,
Napoleon great men and popes, and Roosevelt—
All light!   Yuan Chang great man too.
Like Fa Hsien he go trou Gobi desert,
Fight robbers, dragons, no water, no food;
See much broken cities;
Go from Samarkand to Nepal;
Gone fourteen years;
Come back to Singor,
Tai-tsung emperor now,
And vely glad to see Yuan Chang,
Who bring tousands of books by god Budda,
Gold, silver, crystal images of god Budda,
And bones of god Budda, hair, nails, leaves of Bo tree,
All like that.   Where is Kliste now?   I don't know.
China hear not much. . . .

Tai-tsung great emperor!   Know much too!
Know about Allah, know about Budda,

HIP LUNG *ON* YUAN CHANG

Know about Kliste, and Salvation Army.
But Tai-tsung no give a damn,
Only say to Yuan Chang:
Write Budda books in China language.
And write Lao Tzu in Indian language.
Trade gods that way! We no lose.
Maybe India see more in Lao Tzu
Than China, who knows? All time
Kliste dead more'n six hundred year,
And no body say much bout Kliste,
And China goin' to hell, as Salvation Army say,
Alle time.

Kliste dead six hundred year,
Salvation Army come to England,
And baptize everybody; but China no hear.
Kliste dead eighteen hundred year,
England come to China for Kliste and opium—
Make nice dreams—what you care
'Bout Budda, Kliste—Smoke? Eh?

ULYSSES

Settled to evenings before the doorway
With Telemachus, who sat at his knee,
"Why did you stay so long from Ithaca,
Leaving my mother Penelope?"

The eyes of the hero rolled and wandered,
Thinking of Scylla and Sicily.
"That's a hard question," answered Ulysses,
"Harder, if answered, for you to see.

"There was the Cyclops, there was Æolus,
There were the Sirens, and Hades for me;
Apollo's oxen, Hades' horrors,
Circe, and then Ogygia.

"All these after the war, Telemachus—
Too long a tale, as you will agree.
The bards must write it, when you are older
Read till the gray hairs give you the key

"Of the wonder and richness that were your father's
Life in the war, the long way home.
No man has lived, as I, Telemachus,
None ever will live in the days to come

"A life that followed the paths and hollows
Of Time, the wayward ways of the streams
That flow round earth, the winds and waters
Of passion, wisdom, thought and dreams.

"There are two things, my boy, and only
Two in the world, remember this:
One thing is men, the other women,
And after the two of them nothing is.

"I have known men as king and warrior,
Known them as liegmen, spears of the line.
Good enough lamps for workaday darkness—
They are not food, they are not wine;

"They are not heat that stir the secret
Core of the seed of a man, be sure.
And I, Ulysses, needed the planets,
And suns of the spring to live, mature."

"What do you mean?" asked Telemachus,
"And, say is it true you lost eight years
Away from Ithaca, me and my mother
Because of a certain Calypso's tears?"

The eyes of the hero rolled and wandered.
"There now, my boy, you have the truth.
I'll try to tell you perhaps you'll get it
In spite of your filial love and your youth.

[226]

ULYSSES

"First, understand there are two things only;—
One is women, the other men.
And men I knew before and at Troyland,
And searched their hearts again and again.

"What do you get?   Secrets of cunning,
Cruelty, strength, and much that you use
In the battle with them; but what's a woman?
She is the mother, she is the Muse

"That leads and lifts to life—Telemachus
How can I tell you?—have a care!
Young men seize on the words of wisdom,
And find their hands in a silken snare,

"Hearing blindly, seeing literally,
What is a sword, a lamp, a shield?
Touch and learn, the name is only
The shell wherein the thing is concealed."

"What do you mean?" asked Telemachus.
"What do I mean?   Attend to me!
I'll try to tell you, telling a story
Of the island called Ogygia.

"I know women—how shall I tell you?
Women are good, and good is wine.
Yet how to tell the wine and women
That turn her adorers into swine.

ULYSSES

"You must have aid of Hermes, swiftness
Of spirit and sense to tell them apart;
How to be strong, how to be tender,
How to surrender and keep your heart.

"Easy for me to baffle Circe,
Easy the Sirens to slip—just wax!
I steered for Ithaca, you and your mother,
Isle to isle on the ocean's tracks,

"Until I came and saw Calypso.
Son you would be with Calypso yet.
It takes a hero suppled in flame
To see Calypso, and leave, forget

Face and voice enough to leave her,
Spurn her promises, turn from her tears,
Come to Ithaca with this doorway,
Age that hovers, the little years."

"What do you mean?" asked Telemachus.
"Live and learn," Ulysses replied.
"Calypso promised me youth eternal
If I would stay and make her my bride."

"And why not stay?" asked Telemachus
"To have her for wife, if not a youth
Eternal given you?" "Boy of me listen
Now for the core of the deepest truth:

ULYSSES

"We dined in grottoes of blooming ivy;
We supped in halls of cedar and gold;
We slept on balconies, sapphire tented—
But even I found this growing old.

"I saw her beauty bare by star light,
And by the sea in the sun, and stoled
In silk as white as snow on Parnassus—
But even I found this growing old.

"Her tresses smelt of the blooms of Hymettus,
Her breasts were cymbals sweet to behold;
Her voice was a harp of pearl and silver—
But even I found this growing old.

"Her lips were like the flame of a taper
Scented and musical, as she would fold
White arms over the brawn of my shoulders—
But even I found this growing old.

"She promised me this and youth forever,
So long as the sun and the planets rolled.
I knew they were gifts she could not give me,
Empty promises too grow old.

"And even if given, why forever
Live the things that have grown enough?
She loved me, wonderful Calypso.
But what is love?   It is only love.

"And the salt of a man turns to his doorway,
He makes his will for his blood at the end.
My boy, that's why I left Calypso
And came to you—do you comprehend?

"To sit unshorn, and clothed as I choose,
Talk with the swineherd, potter or shirk,
Babble at ease, my boy, with your mother
Around the house at rest or at work.

"And you must not forget, Telemachus,
In order to have immortality
It had to be with Calypso—therefore
I came to you and Penelope,

"Who soon will leave me, at best, or else
I'll leave you for the Isles of the Blest.
I find this doorway good, Telemachus,
As a place to dream and a place to rest."

"I do not understand, Ulysses,
Father of me.   At first the call
Of the blood, I thought, would hasten you homeward.
And now I wonder you came at all

"Here to Ithaca.   What, my father,
Is here but my mother growing old;
Aged Laertes, Telemachus—
What of Calypso's hair of gold?

"What of the island, what of the feasting,
What of her kisses, were it I
I'd spurn eternal youth, as a mortal
Live with Calypso until I should die."

"I have no doubt," said the many minded
Great Ulysses.   "It's plain to see
You are a boy yet.   When is supper?
Go ask your mother Penelope."

THE PARTY

Our wishes not consulted whether
We chose to come, not even the hour,
Some would have asked for fairer weather
Than on a day of sun and shower.
No chance to choose! And some got wet,
Were sick and nervous while they stayed;
Others came in the sun, the debt
Of Fortune to them overpaid.
We all came ignorant, willy-nilly,
Pell mell, piebald, grave and silly,
Resistless to the party drawn,
Which had gone on and would go on
From dawn to night and night to dawn.
Though some, it seemed, had scarcely come
Before they left; and some at noon,
Or morning bade adieu. The moon
Saw others take departure home.
All talked about it as you would;
Esteemed it dull, over too soon,—
Bad, sad, or wearing, very good!

Over too soon! Yet truth to tell
It was a lasting festival.
Guests had to leave—and that was all.
To each some different thing befell.

THE PARTY

The party went on just the same.
First guests departed, late arrived;
Fresh candles burned with brighter flame;
New cakes were cut, and laughter thrived
Over a wit re-sharpened. Crumbs
Of eaten things were brushed away;
Dishes were cleared and lovelier bowls
Were piled with new picked grapes and plums.
The place the while was mad and gay
Because of sad and merry souls.
There was a room for love's romancing;
A room for talk, a room for dancing;
A room for globes and maps and books;
A room with sky lights, a room of nooks;
A room of pictures, marbles, bronzes;
Guns, gauntlets, spears, armor, sconces;
A room of racks and torture hooks;
A room of ikons, shrines and josses;
A room of crosiers, cups and crosses;
A room—but everything was here—
That brain can think of, plan or make
To shackle spirits, honor brows,
To thrill the heart, or start the tear,
Or stir a rapture, or an ache—
It was a wonder house!

I noticed this: You enter with
Fellow arrivers, ill at ease.
The rooms are full, and some of these

THE PARTY

Know you, but only with their eyes
Acknowledge you in mild surprise.
Listen! and you will get the pith
And meaning of what went before
From these. The high ones talk in myth,
Who own the rooms—in loose ellipsis
Show what their tried out fellowships'
Inner communion is and lore.
But kinder souls say: "Some one great
Was here before you came." "This thing
Happened this morning." "Look! that one
Just going out, is so and so."
"There comes the waiter with your plate!"
"You should have heard that woman sing!
She's going!" "Oh, we've had such fun."
"What happened? What's ahead? It's slow!"
Late stayers stare your ignorance:
"Why don't they tell us?" "Oh, no use,
You wouldn't understand. You'll know
Later, perhaps, by happy chance.
And if you don't, it's too abstruse,
We have no words. Feed on and run
The rooms around. You'll see what we
Have felt, seen, suffered and enjoyed."

And so it is to father and son,
Mother and maid. Then what should be?
The bell rings, some are glad, annoyed:
New guests are coming, and for some

[234]

THE PARTY

The Chauffeur rings, the Car has come!
And we who were the novices,
And wondered, stared, deferred, inquired,
Are now in charge, and take amiss
Curious questions, have acquired
The Party's manner, secrets, speech.
And see, as those before us saw,
New and old groups are troubled, each
Is deaf and dumb.   How can we draw
Their wordless wonder to the point?
What would you know?   How can we reach
And vocalize your dumbness?   What
To ask of us you do not know,
And what to tell you we know not—
Groups, therefore, clearly out of joint.

Yes, but they do not know us now.
Most here are strange.   Where is the throng
With whom we came?   Where is the brow
Sunny of hair, the voice of song?
Where is the hand that understood,
Without a word?   There's none to hear,
And know our meaning as he would . . .
New wine is opened.   No more wine!
New cake is cut.   I must instead
Drink brandy, bitters, heavy beer.
I rather like this coarse, black bread.
Strange music plays, not high and clear.
No matter!   For you might inspect

[235]

THE PARTY

The pictures, marbles, once again,
Look at the books some more, correct
First errors. Surely that were well.
And you can do it, having fared
So differently. Was that the bell?
"Your chauffeur's here!" "Why speed me so?"
"Too bad! Too bad you have to go!"

Yes, but the party's over! No?
Over for me. And I am tired.
Desire for what I once desired
Is dying or is satisfied.
Tell him to wait a moment—yes
I wish to see what may betide;
Watch the new comers laugh and feast;
Watch eyes that glance, and breasts that heave;
Watch cunning, aspiration, pride;
Watch soldier, statesman, poet, priest;
Watch those who doubt and who believe,
Untangle, tangle, spin and weave.
I've helped to make the party, still
The party is not to my will.
I can re-make it, now I know
How to enjoy it better, use
Its hour more wisely. "By your leave.
Just wait a moment!" "Well, your car
Is at the door and must not park;
The way you go is rather far,
Besides it's growing dark."

THE PARTY

Bowed out! No matter! I am due
At a better party, so they say.
To-morrow is a better day—
Always to-morrow. "What of you?
You're coming? Well, I hope you may."
"Meantime good night, a safe return,
And blessings on your way."

CELSUS AT HADRIAN'S VILLA

This is the place, my friend Aristo. Here
We sit and muse on the state of the world. Alas!
What are we coming to?

                    The tufa walls
Inlaid with yellow lichens look like bronze
Gold filagreed. And through those rifts and breaks
There are the trunks of ilex, gnarled and dark.
Look! Nature mocks us. Hadrian is asleep
These nearly hundred years. Does cyclamen
Crimson about these walls grow less profuse?
Or these anemones laugh less to the sun?
Or bramble, honeysuckle, bougainvillea
Desert the gardens of the emperor?
The merle and golden-crested wrens build nests,
Sing the hymeneal song! But man, poor man,
Forsakes his triumphs, work, his palaces.
And barbarous weeds sprout over them and creep,
And choke his wisdom and his art.

                      Let's sit
Here in this colonnade. Philosophers
From Rome and Athens, Alexandria,
From mystic India, walked this colonnade,

CELSUS AT HADRIAN'S VILLA

And let the mind run free. It is no more,
Unless we fight the human weeds that spring
Under the rains that darken Rome. Let's up
With hoes and root them.

                      Here's cat-brier—chop!
Cat-brier, Christian meekness, fair to view—
But how it stinks! And briars: pain and loss
For ecstasy and gain beyond—I chop!
Chop here, Aristo, get your friends to chop,
Lest all the world be given up to weeds,
As Hadrian's Villa is about to be.
Rome soon will stretch her templed neck to breathe
Above the thorns, the hyssop. Even now
The state is crumbling with the heresy
That Rome should not be reverenced and saved,
But every soul saved. The Imperial City
To which each Roman is a servitor
Put by for doctrine making every heart
Worthy of saving from the wreck of life—
I chop this weed. And for the soul of Rome,
The lazar soul, the slave, the fuller, cobbler,
The fool, the God-forsaken and the child . . .
What if Rome fall? The City of God remains
Eternal in the Heavens. Yes, but Earth,
Where is thy city, if it be not Rome?
Destroy your Romans, Hadrians, what is left?—
Itinerant exorcists and prophets, idlers,
And sacred beggars, leper lips that curse

CELSUS AT HADRIAN'S VILLA

Rome and her beauty! These the citizens
Of the City of God! What will that city be?
Themselves externalized, as Rome has flowered
From Roman minds; but never a Hadrian Villa
In the City of God, never from scowls and sores!
No! You shall have a world of trade and lies,
Of itching and denials, for a world
Of freedom and expression, wine and song.
These huckstering Jews are planting in our Rome
The faith that they persuaded God to kill
His Son to save them. And a huckstering
Will taint the flesh of all who eat this god.
But yet how they will rub their palms and coo
And ape a meekness. Here! Aristo, chop! . . .

But just so long as stones remain in place
Of Hadrian's Villa, eyes will look upon them
And sense the mind of Rome, and what it was:
That eyes were made for seeing, ears for hearing,
Hands made to touch, tongues made to taste, minds made
To think, imagine, love given to indulge
For rapture. There's no law of heaven or earth
That trims eyes, ears, the senses,
Of use; but all were made to leaf and bloom
The idea of the eye, the ear, the hand.
And only reason with regard for health
Of eyes, ears, hands, may guide and say: how far. . . .
See now what Hadrian's mind created here:—
A tragic theatre, a comic theatre.

CELSUS AT HADRIAN'S VILLA

What for? For eyes' sake, for exploring life.
Katharsis? Yes. But use? No use to him
Who thinks life sin, the world's end near, for Jews
Who like the frogs in marshes croaking, say:
"For our sakes was the world created, we
Alone are chosen of God." No use for him
Who sees enough of suffering in life
Without its mimicry; sees not the art
Of shooting light between the mystery
Of human fate, and waking sympathy
Through understanding. Christian weeds I chop,
Whose roots begin to sap the tragic roots
Of Sophocles.

            But I say eyes may see:
And if I wish to watch the lions fight
What interdicts me, and what reason for it?
Now look how Hadrian's mind puts into flower:
A temple for Greek books, and one for Latin;
And there's the stadium, and there's the baths.
These Christians frown the bath. If I make out
Jesus may come today, and wherefore wash?
Besides the naked bathers cling and kiss
Within the tepidarium at times, and hence
Out with all bathing!

                There's the palace too
Which o'ertops Nero's Golden House, they say.
And what guest chambers here! The laughing soul

CELSUS AT HADRIAN'S VILLA

Of Hadrian glows amid his friends. What's best
In life, Aristo? Why, when the soul is freed,
From business, traffic, grasping, thought of self,
The aches of the day, and being freed shines forth
As star companions star, in smiles and words
Of praise, affection. Hadrian loves the faith
Of happiness, and lets his guests fare free,
Wander eight miles of garden, enter vales
Of Tempe, watch a mimic Peneus
Flow by; encounter fauns amid the brakes;
Surprise Bacchantes sleeping; hear from hills
A chorus of Euripides soothe their souls
With dreams before Faustina's sculptured face,
Or Antinous, Apollo, Venus; bathe
Their glowing bodies in the pools; partake
Of food or wine, gifts of the gods. Such life
Is passing, soon will pass. Aurelius
Lies under thought, which thrived before the day
Of Paul for all of that, the folly sees not
Of slaying Christians, while himself is teaching
The Christian doctrine! Ugliness, denial,
Self-laceration, beggary, are older
Than Jesus—and I chop!

                              But let the world
Submit to weeds, in time what will you have?
Not Hadrian's Villa, but a villa walled,
Walls spiked and guarded, and a house of walls
Empty of sculpture, where a miser-man,

CELSUS AT HADRIAN'S VILLA

Guarding his gold, a lone man eating bread
And milk, rules realms and countries from the book
Of Enoch, Exodus, the Septuagint,
And these purported writings of one Paul;
And who has made his heart a granary
For seed of faith and trade. This weed I chop!
For then your world lies flatter than the land
Of that campagna, made a marsh for frogs,
Dull grass and feculent roots, as it would lie
If once invaders smashed the aqueducts
And drowned our lovely plain!

                      You see, my friend
Why I fight back the weeds. This is not all,
For I know what engenders Christian faith:
Man dreams he can be saved, but saved from what?
Sin? What is sin? Age? What can save from age,
What keep the spring of youth, its rosy flesh,
Its spirit never tiring, hope undarkened,
Its courage without fears, long dreams and days?
Why nothing! All's illusion that holds forth
A medicine for wrinkles, shrunken arms.
Therefore what saves from death? Does Jesus save?
Does Jesus ease a soul's pain, cure a loss
Save as these devotees may soothe their hearts
With prospects of to-morrow, or of heaven?
No! good Aristo, all this Roman realm,
Washed by this sea, for centuries has been
As fertile as the valley of the Nile

For seed of this salvation dream, the seed
Of Mithra and Osiris, Krishna, Budda,
Adonis, Tammuz, Dionysus, Attis,
What is this seed of Jesus? Nothing new:
The virgin birth? That's old as human dreams.
There's Dionysus born of Semele,
A virgin, and of Zeus; great Dionysus
The resurrection of the year, the mad
Intoxicating power of nature, wine.
There is a myth that Jesus at a feast
Turned water into wine, a Bacchic feat.
One myth blends in another like mosaics
Of microscopic jewels. I go on.
Zeus fathers many sons of virgins born,
Is not content with one. He takes Danæ
And Perseus is the fruit, who siays the Gorgons
And saves Andromeda, the human soul.
Devaki is a virgin, weds Vishnu,
And Krishna comes. A virgin is the mother
Of Budda. Horus springs from virgin Isis,
Our Lady, Queen of Heaven, Star of the Sea,
Mother of God, so called for centuries
Before the days of Mary. Neith, the virgin,
Was mother of Osiris. Mithra's born
Of a virgin mother.

                This is what I mean
By fertile soil of Egypt, Persia, Greece,
That crops the seed of Jesus. Is this all?

CELSUS AT HADRIAN'S VILLA

All saviours tally fully. All were born
In caves or stables, chambers under ground;
All labored for the welfare of the race;
All were light bringers, healers, mediators
Between the gods and men. All fell in death,
Descended to the underworld. All rose
To strive for men in heaven; all created
Communions, churches, rites of water, wine,
Last suppers, brought the entheos, spilt their blood;
God, Krishna, Dionysus, Hercules.
And as for that Tammuz was crucified,
Prometheus was nailed and chained.

                                    You know!
These from the mysteries of the heart, from life;—
Death of the year, birth of the year, the hope
That shines amid the mist of doubts and days;
The dream that says if nature leave the grave
Of winter, what's the life of man, to be
Shut from the law that wakes the fallen seed?
If God renews the wine, I drink the juice
Of the grape and live! If God be in the bull,
And must be, life is life, and all is life
Of one divinity, I drink the blood,
I wash therein, cleanse sin, and celebrate
A ritual of salvation, endless life! . . .
I trace all Krishnas, Mithras in this god,
Hope's latest dream.

CELSUS AT HADRIAN'S VILLA

                              What's needed but a flame
That draws these older flames?   What but a man
Of inspiration, labor, sacrifice,
A poet, hater of the scurvy times,
Killed for his blasting eyes, accusing tongue,
To have your Christos?   Jesus lived.   Why not?
'Tis credible; killed by the Jews, why not?
And made a sacrifice for many—doctrine
World old and wide.   From Babylon the Jews
Brought Hammurapi, brought Sacaea too,
A ritual for prisoners doomed to die,
By which they would be decked in kingly robes,
Stripped, scourged and hanged even as we have done
At Saturnalia.   How else "King of the Jews,"
Except by ancient custom?   Think, Aristo,
Would great Tiberius suffer such sedition
Except as drama and in mockery?
Aristo, if this Jesus were the god
As Mithra, Dionysus are, 'twere well
With Rome and Hadrian's Villa.   Understand
If these infatuate zealots, Jews would keep
Their god, belief, but still conform to Rome,
Rome's gods, the empire reverence, who would care?
No Roman!   No one!   But to hear these prophets
Cry through our cities, camps: to everlasting
Flames commit our cities and our lands,
And curse us out of Jewish scriptures, draw
The imprecations of the epileptic
Paul upon us, this I fight, I chop!

CELSUS AT HADRIAN'S VILLA

I stand with sword against the enervation
Of private judgment, that the common man
Is heaven's prize. This demos mania
And ruin of the empire I oppose.
And when these plagues of Christians grow too loud,
And Rome arouses, wants the lions fed,
Or crosses painted with a little red,
I go to see. These anarch colleges,
Illicit schools, called churches, quiet down
When in the circus Christian bones are crunched. . . .

Now for my consolation if Rome fall;
If lowliness and other worldiness;
If meekness, sacrifice; if life's denial;
If all this creed out of inverted thought,
Shame for the lust of life, the Orient's
Sick perfume, drugs, if all of this be taken
Into the body of Rome, the world; the poison
Of Jesus swallowed—this my consolation:
Life, being God, is stronger than God's Son;
Life will digest it, and evacuate
What cannot be digested, and retain
What can be used. Another Rome will rise
If our Rome fall. Let's go up there, a while,
And watch the waterfalls, and have some wine.

INVOCATION TO THE GODS

I

Goddess, born of the mother of all things, the sea,
Goddess of beauty, goddess of rapture,
Goddess whose girdle is life,
Come down to us, O Aphrodite.
We are sunk in the slough of our shame;
We are torn with denials and fears,
Who have turned from thy altar,
And rejected thy worship
And mangled the gift of love
For the ritual of Mary the Virgin.
Come down to us that we may re-make ourselves
In the likeness of thy face—
We have no goddess like thee
O Aphrodite!

II

And thou, equal sister, O goddess
Whose temple yet stands enthroned rock-bound above
The grotto of Mary of Galilee,
Eternal symbol!
Come down to us:

[248]

INVOCATION TO THE GODS

Preserver of the state
In peace and war,
With the healing of harmonious thought.
Stern goddess of an equal law,
And ruler of the mind.
Guardian of temples and republics.
Lover and inspirer of the arts,
Come down to us that we may re-make ourselves
In the likeness of thy face.
We have no goddess like thee
Pallas Athena!

III

Thou soul of the Sun
And master of fire,
Law-giver, ruler, warder,
Founder of templed cities,
Founder of states invincible and free;
Thou voice of prophecy, wisest friend
Of commonwealths;
Lord of music, lord of words and sounds,
And brother of the muses.
Come down that we may re-make ourselves
In the likeness of thy face.
We have no god like thee
O great Apollo!

IV

Of old amid the mountains sat the father
Of gods and men!

INVOCATION TO THE GODS

Broad souled as nature, being nature.
Human and gracious, laughing, wise as time.
Ruler of earth and heaven—all but fate;
And promising no life that was not fate;
No wonder and no change
Beyond the rule of fate.
Great Zeus whose fruitful loins
Peopled Olympus
With gods and goddesses, well belovéd.
Not father of one son, but many sons;
Not father of one daughter, but many daughters,
Begotten of thee, immaculately,
Being begotten in nature.
Great father of redeemers who redeemed
Through truth which frees through being known,
Not faith in truth which is not known.
Beauty and not belief,
Mystical waters, curses, flames and death!
Come down, O Father Zeus, while we re-make
Our faces in the likeness of thy face.
We have no god like thee
O sovran Zeus!

V

Thou Thunderer, whose mood was wine and love,
Miraculous life, creativeness
Of color and sound,
Out of the lightning, out of the mist,
Out of the beat and urge of the sea,

INVOCATION TO THE GODS

Out of mountains, sacred groves and streams.
Thou king and father of the virgin daughter
Templed in pure, in deathless stone
In sacred Athens.
Not always striking at the foes of Hellas;
Nor sending fury on her enemies;
Nor bathing swords in heaven
To smite the foes of Hellas;
Nor treading grapes in anger;
Nor sprinkling blood on garments
To make all peoples worship thee, O Zeus!
Nor breeding worms that die not,
To make all peoples worship thee, O Zeus!
Nor stirring envy like a man of war
To make all peoples worship thee, O Zeus!
Nor preaching words of gladness to the meek;
Nor opening prison doors
To sound the day of vengeance,
To make all peoples worship thee, O Zeus!
Nor saying, eat the riches of thy foes,
And suck their milk;
And make them plowmen;
And take dominion over them and power.
I am the one, the only god, go forth
And make all peoples worship, I am Zeus!

VI

The hunted ghost of Delphos steals
From land to land.

INVOCATION TO THE GODS

Thy lyre has been weighed in the balances
Of the money changers, and rejected.
The Prince of Peace has brought the sword
Even as he prophesied.
All peoples are at strife
Between his ritual and the will to life.
Vengeance, hypocrisy and darkness
Are over us, we are vipers
Coiled in a cistern.
We wait for blood in the moon,
For darkness in the Sun,
For a voice from clouds of glory:
Depart from me, accursed; into fire.
I shut the gates of heaven
And burn the world with wrath!

Thou in Olympus tombed
With all thy sons and daughters,
Palace no more, a footstool
For Jehovah of Judea,
Come back that we may re-make ourselves
In the likeness of thy face.
O, father Zeus,
Wake when Jesus shuts
The gates of heaven,
And take us to Olympus!

PENTHEUS IN THESE STATES

I

Muse of the meditative hymn, and Muse
Of chronicles and the scroll, to us refuse
No gift to sing the daimon, the divine
God-head of Nature, Freedom and the Vine.
Nor less that Orpheus of the Mysteries:
Stars and the Soul and Heaven, and the Seas
Of tangible streams made light above the dust
Of this bewildering earth of Flesh and Lust.

II

First from what Thracian land
Did your attendants come
In coon-skin caps and jeans,
Into this wilderness, spanned
By mountains, to this home
Of the Corn-mother, clothed in variable greens
Of barley, oats and wheat?
Hither hurried your adventurous feet
From England, and from the hills
Above the Rhine, and out of the valleys
Of the populous plain

[253]

PENTHEUS IN THESE STATES

Of Lombardy, around the Seine,
You came
Like flame that follows flame!
From Galway, Lyons, Bergen, Budapest,
Onward you pressed,
With hearts that sang, and brave,
Like wave that runs to wave!
And from all northlands of new dreams, from ills
That stir the Spring awakening and the quest.
Thence were these swarming sallies
Into New England, and the great Northwest—
Virginia and Kentucky, Tennessee.
Thracians you were, attending Dionyse,
And seeking realms of Nature to be free.
Ciders from orchards would have ease,
And wine from vineyards, to be planted,
Where the roar of mountain torrents haunted
Heights of the pine and slopes of fragrant grasses
From plains to granite passes.
Rocks sealed with frost and ice which prisoned
The secret wine of Life new sensed and newly visioned
Flowed when the Spring of a great Age, and its Herakles,
Fire of the Sun of Liberty, melted the locks
Of ancient and forbidding rocks
Binding the torrent: human and divine
Strength and adventure: Mænads and Thyiades,
Bacchæ, Bassarides:
Spirits and evangels of new wine.
Mad Ones: armed for war.

[254]

And Rushing Ones: defying Strife.
Inspired Ones: trailing the Star
Of larger life.

III

And with this swift descent,
To this far occident,
Tracking the gleam, the god, the freer fields;
Rejoicing, but in rites
For the Mystery, the delights
Of living and of thought, which moulds and wields,
These hunters, fur-capped, like the devotees
Out of the Thrace of old, worshipping and defending
The wine-grower, and temple-builder, Dionyse,
Carved from the fire impregnate Earth the sovereignties
Of Maryland, New York, and Tennessee's
Mountainous realm, to the blending
Of foothills with the meadows of Illinois.
And made initiate in great liberties
The farthest West, until the Orient sea's
Soft thunder lustrates California, bending
Above green water, clothed in purple and gold.
Carved these with hope their children would uphold,
And no hand would destroy
The altars of States heaped full of grapes and grain:
Births of the Sun and earth, to be adored,
And gathered in high festival and joy
From mountain side and plain;
And drunk from golden kantharoi,

PENTHEUS IN THESE STATES

God entering into man, thereby: restored
By the blood and flesh of the god, the lord,
To strength and vision to unveil
Deep mysteries and raptures, worshippings
Of nature, love for man, for deities
Quick intimations, quiverings through the wings
Of larger life, and sweeter music, cities
Of higher fellowships and lovelier ways
Of wisdom, where the phantoms of the Pities,
And the Hatreds, the Agonies
Of Melancholy, Madness, Soul's Disease
From horrors, and from idiot pieties
Are softened or dispelled in Freedom's praise.

IV

Pentheus in the tree-top spies upon
The wild white women, the dance, the festival.
And Judas spies on Jesus
In the epiphany of Orpheus out of Dionysus.
But the cup is drunk by the lover, the singer John.
Who finding the ecstasy of sorrow, and sounding the deeps
Of love and vision, human and mystical
In the wine cup, oh, beloved guest,
Sinks in a moment of ineffable rest,
And rid of the flesh, half sleeps
Upon the Master's breast.
Judas alert for treasure and for treason
Dips in the sop his bread—
Judas the founder of the sect which fouls

PENTHEUS IN THESE STATES

The feast of Life, lizards and owls.
But where the liknon is borne, the cradle heaped
With fruits and flowers at the bridal feast,
O, Dionysiac Christ, you passed the cup;
And at the supper of parting, O lovely priest,
At the time of the fan, and the purging of the floor,
You served the blood of the grape, and you did sup
With fur-capped fellows, and revealed the lore
Of remembrance for the mysteries you had spoken
Over the purple hills, and by the yellow shore
In wine quaffed and bread broken.

V

Thin lips where cruel smiles betray
Envy and frigid spirits, souls of gray
Who will descend upon you, rend and slay?
Unknowers of the cycle of Man's day:
That nourished flesh grows spirit, and that wine
Is the oil of the lamp of the soul, and feeds the flame
That lights the world with Art! Who will waylay
Your spying and your hatred, limb from limb
Tear you, or drive you to a death of shame,
Like Judas self-hung? As if in paradigm,
Purple but horrible! Cut-throats of the rites
Of amity and dreams, the blossoming,
The release from the flesh to soul's delights,
Intenser life in soft intoxication—
And from that life, and rapturous elation
Who are you who restrain,

PENTHEUS IN THESE STATES

Making a cult of undelivered pain?—
Through which men love and fashion, sing.
You false salvationists and street haranguers,
Self-drunk with soul suppression and perversion,
Who shout the terror of putrescence, never beauty;
You with suspicions of the peasant Persian;
You foul-breathed ranters of Duty
About these states, you vermin-eaten clangers
Of hog-ribs, paper tambourines:—
Degenerate instruments for an imbecile faith,
And mockeries of bright silver (touched by queens,
The Muses), and the ebony crotola.
You scare-crows of the Mænads and the Muses,
Breastless or babeless women who would vote
For rulership of other homes, not yours.
And you who moralize and gloat
On the refuse of banquets in the sewers.
You preachers of Denial and of Death,
And maniacs of repression which refuses
The cup of life! And in this bacchanalia,
You followers of Orpheus, as reformer,
Plain dressed in alpaca and string ties,
Who bellow forth your prophecies and curses
Not that man lives, but that man dies.
You carriers of umbrellas, not the thyrsos,
Or rifles of the fur-capped pioneers;
Slick spouters who fill fat penurious purses
Out of inevitable tears.
You Judases to Beauty, the sneak, informer,

PENTHEUS IN THESE STATES

Blind that all Canas must precede
The soul's Gethsemanes, that there can be
Save Cana strengthens, no Gethsemane;
And if no living then no heart to bleed
Its blood to make us like the god, the Christ.
No flower of spirit without root and vine,
Nor loveliness for our sakes sacrificed;
No beauty without wine—
You who these mysteries see not, or gainsay
Who will tear limb from limb of you and slay?

VI

You who behold no spirit in earth and sun,
And in their marriage no symbol of increase;
And you who plan or plot or brood, but run
About the wine press never, and who shun
The kinship which makes one of beasts and man,
Blossoms and vines and trees.
You who see not the mystery of food,
The ecstasy of the feast, replenishment
Of spirit in the wine-cup, and who ban
In fear or loathing, swooning of the blood;
You who can take as memory's sacrament
The wafer and the thimble of vapid juice,
And yet deny us, seekers of elation,
Re-birth through Dionysus, the youthful Christ:
Living, rejoicing in Life's thrilling spring,
Not grieving in its autumn and decline,
Bridal, not funeral wine

[259]

PENTHEUS IN THESE STATES

In the hour of memory and of parting;
You who forbid our ritual and our use
Of Nature's secrets, our illumination,
        Our sleep, our peace,
Our freedom from the Fears, intoxication
        In which our souls are paradised;
Our insight, charities, and our release
        From the grave of the day's flesh, our Orphic lips
Through which we find creations, sun-lit wings,
Love, wanderings of the soul, and fellowships—
You who these wisdoms see not, or gainsay
Who will tear limb from limb of you, and slay?

Will the old States never come to us, never again,
        And the sovereignty of men,
In the mountains of our fathers, along the boundless
        plain?
Has the will of the people perished, or passed into the
        hand
Of the oafs and boors and lunk-heads of the land,
        And the bigot, Puritan,
And the martyrs to the martyrdom of Pain,
Seeking remembrance not for Life, but Death?
Have we given up the sister realms, the freedom of the
        States
        Through a tyranny of shame
In the South land where the black-man wears the gag?
Shall we bear the blight of cities, charged to electorates
In the silence of the bearers of the flag?

PENTHEUS IN THESE STATES

Shall the cowardice of sycophants commissioned to obey
    Defeat the trust, but call it still our voice?
Shall we who give you, as we wish, the choice
    Of freedom to be solemn or rejoice,
Avenge not your injustice, nor gainsay,
Nor strew you limb from limb along the way?

COMPARATIVE CRIMINALS

Marion Strode, my friend, a chanting voice
For heaven's kingdom on this earth, a hand
Ready to open prisons, heal the bruised,
Bring liberty to men, was wrought to fire
Over the martyrdom of Ott. He called it
A martyrdom, and said: "Come go with me
And comfort Ott in prison." So he went.

And on the train I read what Ott had said,
For which he suffered prison. Jail for words
Is older than Saint Paul; as old as cities,
And fear that dreads the change that words may bring.
I also saw a picture of this Ott:
Head like a billiard ball, a little cracked,
Warped egg-like too. A homeless cat made furtive
By missive cans and frightful hoots. A ragged
Gabriel shut from heaven's bliss. A porter
Of righteousness compelled to open the gate
Of paradise for Mark Hanna, but himself
Debarred an entrance. Asking nothing either,
Yet facing God to sift him, find him pure
As those who enter.

COMPARATIVE CRIMINALS

Here's a man who never
To eighty years loses from brightening eyes
Flames from the stake reflected, or the shadows
Of prison for the sake of conscience. Thinks
No one who has soft raiment ever reads
"The Ancient Lowly," or the "Martyrdom
Of Labor," history, science; none are wise
But radicals.

And then I read in full
What Ott had said for which they prisoned him.
They charged him with obstructing the enlistment.
But in his speech there isn't a single word
Advising a resistance to the draft,
By just so many words concretely. Quite
Adroit this speech, quite foxy. Yet it's true
If you knew you could get a man to act
On what was in his mind, long brooded on
By giving him a shot of alcohol;
And if you gave it and he did the deed
You would be an inciter, principal
And doer of the deed.

Now take this speech
Which glorifies the socialistic cause;
Lauds divers martyrs tried, already jailed
For words against the draft; denounces Prussia,
Oh, yes! but in such words as hit the home
Of the brave, the free America! Ouch! Quit!

COMPARATIVE CRIMINALS

Says that the master class has always made
The wars in which the subject class was used,
Which never had a voice in making war:
Affirmative universal! What's the answer?
He means this war, this holy war, the traitor!
Denounces capital, exhorts the crowd
To strive for something better than to be
Fodder for cannon. What? The prize of death
In battle called a foddering of the cannon!
What better thing to strive for? Throw him out!
The price of coal is due to plutocrats;
They're bleeding you, and say it's for the war.
They lie! What's treason? Not disloyal
To those you work for, but disloyalty
To truth, your better self.

                If you believe this
Would you become a soldier, or say no,
I will not fight for such a cause or country? . . .
I see, said Voltaire, three times one are one.
A man in heat might flout the trinity;
But when he studies out some persiflage
With which to flout it—well—here's Ott who has
Contempt aforethought for the war and draft,
And squirts his venom through closed teeth, the better
To shoot it further, make it hit.

                    I said:
"Your Mr. Ott is guilty of the charge.
No use to talk of constitutions. No.

COMPARATIVE CRIMINALS

He loves the Lovejoys, Garrisons and Paines,
The Brunos, martyrs, let him stand his ground."
And Marion Strode replied: "Yes, Ott is guilty.
But did he speak the truth? Yes? Very well.
It must have been the time and place that made
The penitentiary for twenty years
A fitting penalty. But when's the time
To talk against war's horror? When there's war,
And words are vivid, or when war is not,
And talks against it sound like when you say
'Look out for bears' to children?

                  "War-lords talk
In peace and war to be prepared. May I
Prepare for peace in war time, when my words
Have demonstrations in the events of war?
You think not? The majority has spoken!
Well, has it? Point me out a plebiscite
That asked for war. But take your point at full
The majority has spoken: why forbid
The back-hall, soap-box rostrum; what will come?
The majority will stick and go ahead;
Or else the soap box will persuade it back
And end the war. Is there another term?
The great majority annoyed, obstructed,
Delayed, distracted, harried! Well, you know
The Tories did that to George Washington.
And Lincoln! Why, the people at the polls
Returned a critical congress. And if trials

COMPARATIVE CRIMINALS

Strengthen the character of a man, why not
Obstructions for majorities howling war
To clarify and strengthen them? God works
In ways mysterious, but in every way;
Whatever is is true.

                  "Ott, as I see it,
Was jailed for twenty years for speaking truth
At the wrong time and place. A heavy fine
For wrong æsthetics, etiquette.

                       "I go deeper,
I pass the law that jailed him, all æsthetics,
All etiquette, all wrong of time and place.
Let's enter in a realm of realer things.
What does Ott stand for in a war or peace?
Is it not freedom, equal rights, the end
Of poverty, disease? Has he not held
The torch of science up, the torch of thought
Interpreting the greatest minds to win
Attention to them and adherence to them?
If he did this, has not his life been given
To making America a brighter light,
A sounder realm, her breed a stronger breed?
If he be not a light himself, but only
A humble trimmer of the wick, let's say
The wick of Socrates, or Franklin, Paine,
Or Jesus as the prophet in the work

COMPARATIVE CRIMINALS

Of freeing for the truth, then what of that?
Who gets the judgment in the years to come,
A parlor lamp of yellow flame, that smells
Of coal oil, or your Ott?

                              "Let's take a type:
He woos the average man, appeals to him;
The average man whose morals, art and books
Are just victrola records, microscopic
Echoes of small realities of the past.
He sees what he can do with this America
Of the average man, the common people called.
He follows them and gives them vapid stuff
Of morals, laws and politics.   His aim?
Talk which will win the very largest nod
Of ignorant assent.   Result?   Why look,
He is a daily of a million sale,
He coins the money lecturing, uses too
His following to keep America
Upon the level of the common man
In morals, freedom, thought, virility.
He scoffs at science and the noodles giggle.
Music?   Why, who's Beethoven?   Let me hear
'Lead Kindly Light.'   The drama?   Well, Ben Hur
Is moral and historical.   Sculpture?   Look
At those bronze figures by the mantel clock—
That's Faith and Hope.   Freedom of speech and press?
Within the limits of the law!   And war?

COMPARATIVE CRIMINALS

I loathe it, I opposed it, but when war
Is by the law decreed, I enter too
And howl for what I hissed, for what I called
An evil and a wrong.

           "Now hear me out:
Suppose he could persuade America
To take his books, and music, sculpture, ethics—
That is his purpose, to persuade us all
To take them, as it was the aim of Ott
To stay enlistment and so stop the war—
What of our civilization? It would fall.
If so who should be jailed, this orator
Or Ott?

           "Now we've arrived, can test these souls.
Ott fights the war and sticks, your orator
Opposes the war and quotes the Nazarene.
But does he stick? Why no! The truth remains.
He changes, lifts his nose for noting when
The noses of the majority are lifted.
Our Mr. Ott winters behind the bars.
Our orator retires to Florida;
Emerges slick and strong when April comes
To lecture, get the money.

           "Now suppose
Ott by his talk had balked the war, that crime
Is nothing by the side of the other crime
Of keeping common followers commoner;

COMPARATIVE CRIMINALS

Corrupting thought. The war is over now.
With Ott in prison and the orator out.
Let's test them on the whole, and wholly freed
From war tests; Ott's a trimmer of great wicks;
Your orator a parlor lamp that smells
Of coal oil. And the larger truth would open
The prison doors for Ott, and push the orator
Behind the doors and lock them."

                    Marion Strode
Went on till we arrived. And there was Ott
Serene and smiling in his prison clothes.

                    "We mean
To get a pardon for you," Marion Strode
Spoke out at once, "and give this prison cell
To a certain orator of the commonplace."
Ott laughed and said, "What for? You'd break his
    puerile
And shifty heart. This is a place for men
Who stand their ground. I may not have much brains,
But what I have I use as Socrates
Devoted his. I want to share the greatness
Of the great with what brains I possess. I like
This cell because it helps me do this."

                    Then
We shook the hand of Ott and turned away!

THE GREAT RACE PASSES

They were the fair-haired Achæans,
Who won the Trojan war;
They were the Vikings who sailed to Iceland
And America.
They became the bone of England,
And the fire of Normandy,
And the will of Holland and Germany,
And the builders of America.

Their blood flowed into the veins of David,
And the veins of Jesus,
Homer and Æschylos,
Dante and Michael Angelo,
Alexander and Cæsar,
William of Orange and Washington.
They sang the songs,
They won the wars.

They were chosen for might in battle;
For blue eyes and white flesh,
For clean blood, for strength, for class.
They went to the wars
And left the little breeds
To stay with the women,
Trading and plowing.

THE GREAT RACE PASSES

They perished in battle
All the way along the stretch of centuries,
And left the little breeds to possess the earth—
The Great Race is passing.

They went forth to free peoples,
White and black.
They fought for their own freedom,
And perished.
They founded America,
And perished—
The Great Race is passing.

On State street throngs crowd and push,
Wriggle and writhe like maggots.
Their noses are flat,
Their faces are broad,
Their heads are like gourds,
Their eyes are dull,
Their mouths are open—
The Great Race is passing.

The meek shall inherit the earth:
Crackers and negroes in the South,
Methodists and prohibitionists,
Mongrels and pigmies
Possess the land.
A president sits in a wheel chair
Sick from the fumes of his own idle dreams—
The Great Race is passing.

DEMOS THE DESPOT

Not in the circus before your thumbs inverted,
Demos, the despot, do we stand;
But amid the swarming half-born girted,
And amid the idiot millions who command
Have we our freedom re-asserted—
Rule us you cannot, though you rule the land.

Frederick and Charles and Philip the misbegotten
Destroyed the body with fagots and with fetters,
Until the finger magic of movable letters
Choked them out of a world that they made rotten
With blood and corpses. But, O Demos, you
Plague us with dwarfs that trip us, run and hide;
Foul us with frogs that froth our ancient wine;
Scourge us with locusts, and with snakes that twine,
And hiss but do not kill. With lice subdue
Our patience, and our time divide
In seeking the favored hour. And then you say:
Have you not freedom, pray?
Do you not think and print? You do not bleed
For freedom's sake! You do not die at once.
And if you starve, have you not had your way?
We let you print, but do we have to read?

[272]

DEMOS THE DESPOT

Or suffer what you print to be displayed?
What you call liberty affronts
Our white-frog breasts, the laws we made.
All rightful rights remain.
Neglect and want shall be your ball and chain
If you trespass our rules—
In other times you would be burned or slain!

Such being the freedom that you grant, O Demos,
Our olden task is this: we fire the rushes
Of yesteryear, and beat with sticks of truth
The little snakes and dwarfs that hide in bushes;
Drain the dead water, set exhilarant youth
With ploughs upon the musty marsh to turn
The scum and green decay, and chase the frogs.

Then after we cut and drain and burn
All will be sweet and clean awhile.
But soon the weeds and crawlers will defile
Our labor. Then the demagogues
Will lead the chorus of the frogs:
This is the land, this is the field
This is the age of freedom, long revealed.
This is the age most blest,
This is the country freest, best,
This is the country that fulfills
Ancient hope and prophecy,
This is the age, this is the land,
The land, the age, the realm most free. . . .

DEMOS THE DESPOT

Then in that hour we shall be dancing,
And feasting with new gods upon the hills;
And graving images of lovelier Beauty;
And building altars of a purer Duty;
And singing rituals of a deeper Faith.
And living life, and facing death
As fairer gods would have us. And for you
O frogs, the fated sharers
Of all we dream and do,
We the dreamers, the preparers,
Shall then be gathering strength to burn
Bushes and plow again
The frog marsh and the weedy plain!

A REPUBLIC

Her faith abandoned and her place despised,
Her mission lost through ridicule, hooted forth
From the forum she erected, by cat calls,
And tory sneers and schemes. Her basic law
Scoffed out of court, amended at the need
Of stomachology by the judges, or
A majority of States, as it is said—
Rather by drunks and grafters, for the time
The spokesmen of the States, coerced and scared
By Methodists with a fund to hire spies,
And unearth women scrapes, or other sins
With which to say: "Vote dry, or be exposed."
A marsh Atlantic drifting, towed at last
By pirates into harbor, made a pasture
For alien hatreds, greeds. A shackled press,
And voices gagged, creative spirits frozen,
Obtunded by disgust or fear. War only,
Armies and navies speak the national mind,
And make it move as a man; for other things
Resistance, thought divided, ostracism,
Or jail for their protagonists. At the mast
The cross above the crossbones, in between
The starry banner. A people hatched like chickens:

A REPUBLIC

Of feeble spirit for much intercrossing,
Without vision and without will, incapable
Of lusty revolution whatever right
Is spit upon or taken.   A wriggling mass
Bemused and babbling, trampling private right
As a tyrant tramples it, calling it law
Because it speaks the majority of the mob.
A land that breeds the reformer, the infuriate
Will in the shallow mind, the plague of frogs
That hop into our rooms at Pharaoh's will,
And soil our banquet dishes, hour of joy.
A giantess growing huger, duller of mind,
Her gland pituitary being lost.

THE INN

Low windows in the room
That tunnel the darkness with light!
The tick of a clock in the fog that hovers
From the cave and slide of the darkness
Into the tunnels of light.
A cannon stove, a dog at my feet;
Cheap magazines on a table,
Dead flies, an atlas;
A register for guests,
And stillness! Not a voice, a step—
Only the tick of the clock!

Mists of Fear, Mists of Memory, swirl and writhe,
Dive, curl and coil
From the mountain tops.
A stretch of ochre grass by the river;
Bent trees imploring the sun;
And by the inn a road that stretches
Along the river, full of dead dreams, patience,
Weariness long endured!

Second morning of rain.
Second morning of separation, death in loneliness!

THE INN

The wind rushes to the corner of the porch
And sighs as it hides.
Second morning that I see
The walker of the road:
An opera cloak of blue blows round him,
Flaps out a lining of red.
And an Alpine hat comes down to his little ears.
He is booted, he limps a little.
But he's a figure compacted of iron,
He's master of the landscape;
He has cowed it, kicks it about him,
As if to say: "A village, a road,
A river, mountains, rain, an inn,
And a lonely soul in the inn.
Well, what of it? To-morrow Benares,
To-morrow Bactria—who knows?"

And I know as well as I know dead flies,
And the tick of the clock
He wants me, passes the inn to draw me.
Strides to my view, though he never looks in.
The flap of his cloak is a gesture;
His eyes fixed straight ahead allure.
He is passing again, returns and passes.
I can stand no more!

I walk from the room, and haste to his side.
A rusty hand out of the blue of his cloak
Reaches for mine; silken soft in the palm

THE INN

Like an anthropoid's, but boned
To the strength of bronze in the fingers.
Red scar on his cheek—a sabre cut!
Or was it an aiguille gashed him
When he fell headlong like a meteor,
And rolled to a valley, got up, shook out,
And dusted himself, set forth to travel
From Ctesiphon to Sarajevo? . . .

But now the blue and red,
The Alpine hat, the little ears,
Against the ochre of stricken grass
Are shrunk to the rust of jowl and jaw,
And the scar, like lips grown to;
And the smile of Jenghiz Khan. . . .
His voice is the lowest octave
Of riotous thought, conscienceless as nature.
No talk, much thought. The earth's a treadmill,
And spheres back of us to toes dug in,
Until we come to a mountain lake
Clear and calm as a sky.
Green shadows rich as moss around the shores;
Clouds, clear blues at the centre!
We are bending over, see each other's faces
In the water.
What was it? Red scar on his cheek,
Or red feather in the Alpine hat?
I thrill! For I see his eyes at last;
They are the fires of burning cities,

[279]

THE INN

Carthage, Athens.
Quick! And we are lying
Looking up into the sky.
When a whiff of rotting men—I turn
But he stays me with his hand.
The scent passes—he talks
To me—the sky!

"I am a soul fancier and catcher,
A catcher and cager of birds,
Whether they be kites, condors, cormorants,
Crows, cow-birds, vultures,
Or martins, mocking-birds, or hawks,
Shrikes, orioles, clarindas, thrushes,
Songsters, or scavengers, I catch them,
And in these mountains, call them of memory
Or bitter reflection,
I cage them.
But to be brief: Your bird of prey I catch
By luring him with carrion;
And your mocking bird with sounds
Sweet as his own soul's echo, as it were
Unreal made real. But whether bird of prey,
Or songster, it's to fool them
Always, until my hand cups over so—
Then a cottage, in the mountains of memory!

"I prize the soul called mocking bird
Mimetic of all spirits, would be all,

THE INN

Self-fooler, and world fooler!
Coos in scourged kingdoms like the dove,
Presaging peace;
Croaks like the eagle where the serfs implore
Omens and leadership.
I caught one lately, big as any crow.
And cooped him—you shall see!
But first as far as Prague, borne over seas,
I heard the eagle, yes, was nearly fooled,
Me, the expert in songsters, souls!
I looked my soul-bird up and found
My eagle was a mocking-bird;
And when he croaked of counsel and debate,
And breathing bracing air of matching minds,
He was the mocking bird embowered and hidden
In scented leaves of dreams,
And sang what he would be, but could not be!
A lyrist who sang down seclusion, still
Could live nowhere but in concealment.
A seeker of sweet notes from rich thesauri,
Slaved to the habit of the lexicon.
I would not catch him yet! Believe me now
There is that in each soul which builds its cage,
Achieves its capture, be it thirst or lust,
A lexicon or rhetoric, singing notes
Which makes the world say: 'Hear the eagle cry!'
The world is fooled, but not the self is fooled;
It sleeps, submits to singing, but arouses
When soul is highest charmed with its own song,

And at the apex of the life, and treats
The man as mocking bird for what he is! . . .
The self as mocking bird betrays and leads,
Not eagle-wings, but weak wings to the fray,
And there the realest self is seen at last
Of self and all. To capture them or slay
Is where I come and act.

"Sweet bird of dawning, dreaming of Fourteen,
Who carried Christ across a stream,
And gained the magic sack,
Into the which whatever he wished would come
When saying Artchila and Murtchila.
But, he, this Fourteen, bird of dawning, mock-bird
How could he carry Christ? What magic bag
Would gather in, to words like 'counsel,' 'process'?
So charmed with voice of self he flew alone
To a parley of fowls. And there amid rich crumbs,
Silk vestured falconers, birds of paradise,
Mock eagle fails, but true to song
Utters what self of him destroys him for.
Then I, to end, come in!

"Wouldn't you think he'd know what had been done
To him, his counsels, processes?
Voice of the eagle sometimes, but the talons
And wings, where were they?
How was he Christopherus, how Fourteen?
I step in here and send him

[282]

THE INN

On a great tour of singing, laugh in my sleeve
To see him start with his empty magic bag—
Empty? Great wars to come and woes,
Hatreds and desolations, blight of unfaith,
And distillate of night-shade: Soul's despair
Were in the bag now.
But I forget—all could not see these in it,
Though most could see an empty bag. Well, now
My project was to send him forth to chant
The rhetoric of a life-time, tent him to
The repetend and echo, the refrain
That hides a hollow courage, and a brain
Tired of its make-believe, and borrowed moods.
My plan went further: Thus to send him forth,
And in keen lighting have him see himself
As some ten thousand saw him; in one moment
Together by him and them! flash picture
Photographed on a mountain's wall,
And visible for ages! So it was!
I laughed, but being master I could pity. . . .
My hand goes over him cup-like now, shuts eyes
From sight of how he pecked me peevishly,
Like a stud-sparrow shrilled. Time for the cage
For our mock-eagle, logolyrist, truly!—
You shall know them by their words."

"How's this so quick, on a peak?"
I said, for there we were, and the lake lost.
Below us the plum world, pitted with gums: oceans.

THE INN

Streaked with streams: white-wash excrement of spar-
    rows;
Pine forests: fuzz on the rind; lice green and brown: men.
I bawl in his ear against the breeze
Whirl-pooled around us:
"No Jesus business, no Budda business,
I wouldn't give a damn for it all."
"You lie," he said. "You're like the rest
Esophagus, coil of guts, a vent."
"Man is a spirit." "Man is a smell."
Just then up from the world's valley a breeze
Bearing the stench of ten million corpses—
"Hey! I faint."
I back away, bump into a cottage wall, a door
Which opens—and there
Is logolyrist caged, in durance,
Twittering to himself the habitual notes,
Impotent, damned, alone!

"Night comes quickly these days," says the landlady
Lighting the lamp. I stretch out of sleep
And pat the head of an honest dog.

MONODY ON THE DEATH OF
WILLIAM MARION REEDY

I

Son of the freer Republic, child of a day
More joyous and more vital and more blest
At the feast of Life; great heart, wise and gay,
Forgiving and compassionate, though ever stressed
Between the thorns, seeing afar the flower;
And living from hour to hour
In laughter for your wounds, or with a sigh
For the thickening brambles that around you pressed:—
April has come to me again and May
Since that July
When you sank gladly to a coveted rest,
Almost with your words to me upon your lips:
That immortality
Is not a promise, but a threat; that sleep
However eternal, or however deep
No more the worn out heart equips
For life again; cannot make whole
A liver and a dreamer, and a soul
That climbed, as you did, earth's precipitous steep.

[285]

THE DEATH OF WILLIAM MARION REEDY

II

You who had lived with books and walked the city
Of statesman and of priest,
Of money changer, theorist,
And knew the human heart thereby,
Saw with clairvoyant eye
Behind my irony and laughter, pity;
Behind indifference desire;
At the core of me unquenchable fire,
Walled with impenetrable ice.
This I confess:
I strewed adversities to your love
With pride, with slow forgiveness
Of the world's ways. Yet for the strength thereof,
Born of that mystic brotherhood, which can rise
From kindred spirits, none the less
Was your love mine, even to the end.
You were my brother, O my friend!

III

The wages of Wisdom is Death:—
Shame, Fear, Want, Hate, Lust, Strife and Enmity,
All these you lived, and living them through
You survived them, but still knew
Their quality. At last from them made free
You stood in blossom, perfecter of bloom
At the touch of the sickle than ever in all your years.
Pure flame had conquered the reek and fume

THE DEATH OF WILLIAM MARION REEDY

Of the gross fuel of your nature, feeding
The light that lighted us, but to consume
Itself at last. O soul of eyes and ears
Open and heeding
Signs of all fair and foul in the land, all climes,
Riches of dead epochs, ancient times.
O, human, worldly Augustine, in your tower
Watching the wavering lines of Want or Power,
Hailing and warning, Stilites of the rite
Of Epicurus (that happiness at the last
Is freedom) viewing the misty age
Atop a pillar of Zeus, and holding fast,
Through change and weariness, to work, in spite
Of clear conviction, nothing can assuage
The soul's desire. Though the flesh has food,
And water, and is satisfied,
Yet the soul must hunger for hope, for explanation
Of this insoluble task of life, defied
By every test of the human soul, still wooed
By flitting lights of faith and intimation.
Yet if soul father us could soul not do
For souls of us what water for our thirst
Accomplishes? Promethean, this you knew:
The restless search with which man's soul is cursed;
Yet brooding on it, still you dreamed
Of a city for all nations, consecrate
To the creative spirit of God in man;
Guardian angels were to you revealed
In labor with man's fate,

THE DEATH OF WILLIAM MARION REEDY

Uplifting the human spirit, like a flame,
Consoled, redeemed,
Strengthened and purified and healed,
To the silent, eternal life from whence it came.

III

To this you have gone. I saw your artist hands
That had so little rest
Folded in quietness upon your breast.
Whether the dead find peace, or loose the bands
Of some intenser rhythm, still with peace
Your face was sealed, as of a great surcease:
Like sculpture, tideless streams,
Or winter woods, or windless skies,
Or sleep that has no dreams.
Those spheres of flame, your ever wandering eyes,
Were turned within to a realm more deep,
Where death's great secret seemingly was known
As some clear, mild Simplicity! Or 'twas sleep
Of the unborn that stilled them, or the void
Of the dead seed never sown. . . .
You were no more to me, whatever death is.
I stood alone
Empty of hand, save for the heritage
Of what you were:
A voice, a light, a music of deep tone,
Which life made richer, and the age,
And something of heaven employed
To be for us our best interpreter.

THE DEATH OF WILLIAM MARION REEDY

You were our star of empire lighting
The path of peoples more and more
To a freer day! O, voice of you which woke
Rapt listeners over the earth.
Out of your ashes wings of memory soar
To carry the message of your life and word.
Death of your body was the clearer birth
Of the spirit of you, shining afar
Upon our day and days to be:
As evening winds blow coldly, yet make free
From mist and hovering cloud
The Western Star!

GOD AND MY COUNTRY

He had the bluest eyes I ever saw,
And a smiling face like a bed of yellow daisies,
And a voice around the house like a pet crow.
And he went whistling through the yard and rooms,
His hands grimed up with grease about machines,
Which he could take apart and put together.
And he could run a motor boat or a car.
Or mend a telephone or a dynamo.
And he knew novels, poetry and science.
And he could swim, and box and run a race.
And on a morning I went in his room
And saw his naked body, saw his shoulders
As broad as a great wrestler's, and his arms
As big as mine. He started to play bear,
And took me in his arms and hugged me so
I felt my ribs crack. Then I wondered when
He had quit wearing stockings and knee breeches,
And when it was he slipped to seventeen,
Became a man.

        And so the war came on.
He tried to be a flyer, for he knew
What engines were and all about machines
And he knew trigonometry, and chemistry,

GOD AND MY COUNTRY

And wireless telegraphy—but his age
Debarred him from the flyers; so he chafed
And did not whistle as he used to do,
But growled a little like a yearling bear.
And then his face grew bright again: he had gone,
Enlisted in the army, came to me,
His face all glowing: "Everything I am
You taught to me," he said; "to love the truth,
To love democracy and America.
And now we have a war, the very first
When men could fight to bring democracy.
Our country turned against the revolution
In France, which was a democratic cause,
But now we war to bring democracy
To peoples everywhere, and I am off.
God moves among us, and to serve and die
Are blessings, I am happy, and am off."

He terrified me with his shining face,
His blue eyes, beautiful body, slim and strong.
St. George was not more beautiful. I was awed,
And said to him: "You terrify me, boy.
There are plenty of men to go, await the call;
Go if they call you, but you have your school,
And if you go you'll never go to school
Again, and that will leave you half prepared
For life, you'll feel it all the rest of life."
But he stood up so straight and stern and shining
And said: "I owe this service to you, Dad,

GOD AND MY COUNTRY

For what you've been and taught me, and I owe it
To God and to my country." So it was
He terrified me, and I said: "My boy,
I am not wise enough, after all, to say
What you should do. Perhaps you have a vision—
You are America come to herself;
A vision and a mission and a glory
Perhaps, perhaps. I step aside. Go on!"

They took him to a camp, and in a week
I went to see him. He was in a pen
Like a prize porker, looked a little down.
He had been shot with vaccines of all sorts.
He didn't say much. Two weeks after that
I saw him and he had a cold he caught
From doing picket duty in the rain
And sleeping on a mattress soaked with rain.
The food was pretty good, not very good.
He whispered: "All the pin-heads in the world
Have got the jobs of officers. I'm surprised.
I know more mathematics than they do,
And more of everything. I thought an officer
Was educated. Well, I am surprised."
He said the boys were dying right and left
Because they had no care. And on a day
When he came home to visit for a while
He was stricken with the flu. I telephoned
The officer, who raved and said no trick
Would go with him. He'd send for him. He did,

And took him out with a raging temperature,
And back to camp. He almost died for that.
And, when he got up, wobbled for some weeks.
And about the time he stood up fairly strong
They shipped him off to Europe; and they went
Yelling like tigers smelling blood, and God
Seemed farthest from their thoughts.

                    Well, so it went.
And after while we had the armistice,
The war was over, but no letter came.
Where was he? Dead? We couldn't learn a thing.
Until at last this boy who went to fight
For God and for democracy landed up
In Russia fighting democracy, as America
Fought France in eighteen hundred—for a letter
Came to us telling where he was. And there
He stayed some months and fought for covenants
Arrived at in the open, independence
Of little and big peoples, for the sea's
Freedom, or democracy, I'm not sure,
For one of these or all, I am not sure.
He got through anyway, or they got through
With him, perhaps, for he came back at last,
One eye out and one leg gone, and he'd lost
God, so he said, and didn't use the word
Democracy at all, and, as for war,
He said to me: "What is it? Everything
Has its own idea, and the idea of war

GOD AND MY COUNTRY

Is killing people? That's our job, that's war!
And everybody yells atrocities,
And everybody does 'em—what the hell
Do people think war is, a Sunday School?
I want some money, Dad, for I am broke;
And I can't work at much now, and, by God,
I think I'll write my story. So they'll know
They use you, and they fool you, and you die
That some one may make money selling stuff,
Or grab off lands or commerce. Hell's delight!
When I was sick in Russia, had delusions,
I saw a snake so big he wrapped the world
And swallowed it with everybody in it.
You see, the snake's the money-men, big business,
The schemers, human buzzards, who eat up
Young fellows and the kids, and lay on fat
With fresh young blood that wants to shed itself
For God and truth! I killed a Russian soldier
And said: 'You bastard,' as I stuck him through,
You hate yourself, so you just kill to glut
Your hatred of yourself, your cruelty
Which lusts, as it can masquerade behind
The mask of duty. Give me a dollar, Dad,
To get some cigarettes and some shaving blades."

THE DUNES OF INDIANA

Under a sky as green as a juniper berry
The yellow sands of the dunes, in clefts and curves
Run up and down, until the horizon swerves
At Michigan City, twenty miles from Gary.

Scrawls and grotesqueries of giants who laugh
At the storm's puffed cheeks, the water's pilfering hands!
Like the beat of a heart traced by a cardiograph,
Their sky-line lifts and lulls,
With the eternal pulse
Of air and the sands.

The dunes are a quilt of yellow, green and gray
Spread to the Calumet River.
Peaked by giant children who play
Circus with feet for poles. Fantastic dunes,
Protean hills, and migratory tents
Of invisible gypsies, changing with the moon's
Replenished and exhausted valleys of light.
Forests of pine and oak arise
On many a height,
And down the steep descents
Flourish and vanish from sight,

[295]

THE DUNES OF INDIANA

Under the restless feet of the wandering hills.
They trace in sand the changes of the skies
When the sun of evening smelts
Great towers of cloud or battlements,
And levels them, or warps
Their shapes to broken walls,
Or twisted scraps,
Or floors of emerald strewn with lion pelts. . . .
Here there are water-falls;
Lakes bright as mercury, and pools
Green as the mosses, where hepaticas
And asters scurry before the gesturing wind;
Cool hollows, scented brakes
Of bramble, fern and cane;
Great marshes where the flags leap like green snakes,
Bordered with garish gules
Of pye-weed; over whose wastes the crane
Flaps the slow rhythm of extended wings.
And on whose reeds the blackbird sings
A quaver of blue water, March's fire.

Between the feet of the dunes and the trampling troops
Of waves along the shore the sand is pounded
Into a broad mosaic firm and smooth,
Whereon are strewn old reels, between the groups
Of blackened hut and booth.
Boats lie here where they grounded,
Like skeletons in the desert ribbed and black,
Scaled with the water's scurf.

THE DUNES OF INDIANA

The shore is the moat between the ruined rampart
Of the dunes, whose shifting is stayed
By splotches of thickets, trees and turf,
And the invading surf.
Here phantom mists descend, and the wrack
Of autumn clouds fade into the air when storms
Harry the water, and the sand is flayed
By the whip of the wind.
There is forever here the futile fashioning
Of hills, and their leveling;
The growth of forests and their burial;
Pools filled and rivers changed or dried
Between the spoiling winds, and the mystical
Hands of the tide!

Branches as gnarled as an ancient olive tree
Stream cherry blossoms like blown snow
Toward the blue of the lake, a hundred feet below.
They have been sand, now being blossoms drift
With the winds whose spirit cannot be
Quieted or given shrift.
By night they howl or whine
As if they asked for words, or a sign
To tell of the sand and seeds and spores
Which build and root, bear blossoms, seed,
And change the uplands and the shores;
Destroy, make over, mend
Without use, without end
In an endless cycle of sand and seed,

THE DUNES OF INDIANA

Of wind and the washing of waves;
They would tell why forests grow and find their graves;
And hills glide to their sepulchres,
Even as cities sink and pass away:
Old Memphis, or old Bactria. . . .

NATURE

Seas, mountains, rivers, hills, forests and plains,
Our earth that floats in heaven's translucent sphere,
And keeps us fosterlings, though man attains—
As a spider winds the nerve white gossamer
From its own being, and unwinding sails
The heights—the secrets of the stars, the sheer
Chasms of space, and tears the vaporous veils
From Force and Distance. Nature! At the last
Our breast of consolation! Man exhales
Thereon the spirit which was on him cast
From that same breast at birth. But what you are
Remains, or on the mind of man is glassed
As you, remaining; while the farthest star,
The changing moon, the lessening sun, the sands
Of buried cities toll our calendar
Of dying days. Waters by star light, lands
That slip or climb; leaves, blossoms, fruits contain
The flesh of wonder perished, and the hands
That sought with zeal or laughter, but in pain
To know you and themselves. Still nourishing,
Destroying, but unriddled, you remain!

Immeasurable Arc! To which our brief existence
Is a point, if relative, not understood.

NATURE

With you endowed with motion and persistence,
Contained within you, is life evil, good?
Is life not of you? Is there aught without
By which to judge this restless brotherhood
Of will and water, and to quiet doubt
That life is good? And may the scheme deny
Itself when it is all, and rules throughout,
Knows no defeat, except as forces vie
Within it, striving? But, O Nature, you
Mother of suns and systems, what can lie
As God beyond you, making you untrue
To larger truth or being? You are all!
And man who moves within you may imbrue
His hands in war, or famine on him fall
Out of your eyeless genius, yet what wrong
Is wrought to your creating, magical
Renewal, scheme? What arbiter more strong
Than you are judges discord for the strife
That stirs upon our earth, wherever throng
Thoughts, forces, fires. What is evil? Life!
Even as life is struggle, whether it smite,
Or lift, as waves to waves in will are rife
With enmity. Whatever is, is right.
Like insects on a drift weed water tossed
The sea of nature moves in man's despite,
While generations flourish and are lost.

Ether of the ethereal energy
Which whirls the atoms: Will in man. And soul

NATURE

Which is to light as light to flame: the free
Soaring of man's thought. This is the dole
And tragedy of man: He has outgrown
His kinship with the beasts that kept him whole,
Through thought, which is not instinct, but would own
The unerring realm of instinct. Like a sun
He flares his thought in storms of fire, has flown
His symmetry and sphere, has wandered, won
No orbit for the beast's, which he has marred,
Departed from; must finish what's begun,
Until he be in spirit moved and starred,
Instinct regained to thought, his sun created
As far as flames have leaped; or leave the scarred
Black cavities of his hopes to beings fated
To grow therefrom to what he failed to reach.
Something within him drew the gods, and mated
His spirit to celestial powers. The breach
Between him and the beast is fixed. He sinks
In tangled madness, anger, railing speech,
Below the ape, or else he rises, links
His being to a life to which he climbs,
A realm of thought harmonious, while he thinks.
This is the tragedy of man, and Time's
Colossal task laid on him: Roll he must
The stone up to the peak against the slimes,
And fasten it, or let it make him dust,
Escaped his hand and crushing, still confess
That you, O Mighty Mother, still are just
Who fling him down to failure, nothingness.

NATURE

This is the tragedy of man: to learn
Your secret wishes, having learned to press
The heights of life, or ignorant still to burn
With questioning; and on this stage of earth
Live as they lived of old in a return,
Endless of useless labor, madder mirth.

Labor or Mirth! No matter—but to man,
And for an hour! And after that the sleep.
Waking or sleeping man fulfills the plan
Of you, O Mother. Other thought may creep
On man's defeated spirit, make him say
That you should weep, O Mother, if he weep.
But we are but ephemera in a play
Of tangled sun light, and the universe
Of ages counts the minutes of our day,
And makes them of the ages. And the curse
That man deems his is not upon the far
And infinite existence. It could nurse
No evil in great spaces, sun and star
As great as man's to man, and not lie down
To death as man does. Hence if you unbar
To us, O Nature, nothing better, crown
Our hour with folly still, you give us rest
Among the mountains, meadows, and unclown
Our idiot brows, and on your infinite breast
Rock us eternally under the infinite sky.

THE END